Beginner +

Intermediate

Guide to

Ceramic Glazing

book has been derived from various sources. Please consult a licensed professional before attempting any techniques outlined in this book.

By reading this document, the reader agrees that under no circumstances is the author responsible for any losses, direct or indirect, that are incurred as a result of the use of information contained within this document, including, but not limited to, errors, omissions, or inaccuracies.

Table of Contents

Ceramic Glazing for Beginners

<hr>

What Every Ceramic Artist Should Know to Get Better Glazes

<hr>

Introduction

Making ceramics is a diverse art form that goes back thousands of years and has long played a big role in several cultures around the world. Even when you take a quick look back in history, you will see ancient people producing or trading them. Some items also have an area in museums dedicated to them.

The thing is, working with clay is a time-consuming process that requires many steps. You need to know what type of clay to use, what shape it should hold, how hot the fire should be and where it needs to come from, etc. After all of that, you have to deal with the final and most critical step: glazing.

Glazing is a process that a lot of beginners tend to have a lot of issues with. When you are not used to it, you may end up coating your ceramic with too little or too much of it. Some ingredients may not always be available either, thus making a few recipes impossible to follow. The level of cleanliness that it requires is no joke as well, considering no one wants to see bubbles or bumps on their ceramics. Thus, it is safe to say that glaze can either bring your artwork to a new level of beauty or ruin your project completely and waste weeks of hard work.

The silver lining is that this book focuses on this final step. You do not have to try glazing blindly for the first time and hope that the recipes will work. This book will help you improve your glazing skills and judgment so that you can attain better glazes for your ceramic projects in the future

Chapter 1
The Basics

As mentioned above, the glaze can either make or break your ceramic work. It is important to put time and effort into planning your glaze before applying it, especially how you want the glaze to look and what its purpose is.

This chapter holds some basic information that will help you understand how glazes work and what they do.

What Is a Glaze?

A ceramic glaze is a strong, usually transparent, coating applied to the ceramic work as the final layer. This layer is baked directly into the clay used for ceramics. A glaze has various purposes and qualities depending on the type, which needs to be chosen carefully in connection with what you want out of your final product.

The main purpose of a glaze is to strengthen and waterproof your ceramic. Furthermore, a glaze will give it a rounded look, seal in paints, and even create interesting effects. In most cases, a clear glaze is used, but glazes are available in a myriad of colors. They can also range from extremely reflective to nearly or completely matte.

Glaze Chemistry

The glaze is in liquid form, but long exposure to oxygen and low heat will eventually dry the glaze. To gain a strong, glass-like protective glaze, much higher temperatures are required. The ingredients in different recipes provide a specific combination of oxides and minerals that set off a chemical reaction when exposed to intense temperatures to harden and crystallize. The specific combination of oxides within a glaze will determine the reaction and its final properties, such as strength, color, thickness, and ability to reflect or refract light. The oxides will also ascertain the ideal temperature at which the glaze should be fired and the amount of time it should be exposed to the heat, as well as the resulting color once the glaze is dry. This is an important element when it comes to mixing your own glaze or altering a recipe as a change in the chemical balance can produce unexpected pigments. A basic understanding of which types of minerals make which colors can help you substitute rare or expensive ingredients or change the glaze color.

The Glazing Process

Glazing a ceramic project is a process, not just a single step. The first part begins with planning. It's important to plan what you want to do with your glaze, which colors you want, how transparent it should be, what effects it should have, etc. All of this can influence the choices that you make during the whole procedure of doing your work. Different glazes work better with different types of clay, and the final purpose of your project will also influence your glaze type. For instance, if you make an earthenware pot to prepare or serve food, you need a much tougher glaze with a higher melting point than if you want a purely decorative piece. As the glaze is such a crucial part that can determine the success of your piece, you should put a lot of time and effort into planning and give it careful thought and consideration.

Once you have decided on what you want to do and chosen your clay, you can begin with your project. Because the most common form of ceramics is pottery, this book will explain the glazing process by making a pot as an example.

Pot Making

Without the pot, there is nothing to glaze. Making one is a long process, but it can be summed up in a few basic steps.

The first step involves preparing and mixing different types of clay until you have the desired consistency and texture. Then, you need to work all the air bubbles out of your clay as they can cause structural flaws and weaknesses in your pot.

The second step is forming your pot. There are various techniques that you can use to form your clay into your desired shape, each with their specific requirements and results. Other than your basic shapes, you can add embellishments, such as handles, carve patterns, or pinch your clay.

Once you are happy with the shape and texture of your pot, the next step is to let it dry. Keep your pot in a dry space with good airflow and make sure that no damaging influences, such as children or pets, can reach it. Drying it naturally can take days and even weeks, depending on the type and thickness of the clay, as well as the size of your pot.

An optional step is to go back to your pot after one or two days when the clay should be about as hard as leather. Trim the pot and add more carving decorations, which can risk the structure of the pot if the clay is still wet. After that, it is time to let it dry completely.

Now that your pot is shaped, dried, and decorated, it is time to prepare for the glaze.

Bisque Firing

This step is another optional thing, but it can be of great help to strengthen the pot. The technique requires you to fire the pot in a kiln at high temperatures to set the shape permanently. The temperature for bisque firing is not as high as when firing the glaze, and the pot is not vitrified yet, but this step makes it easier to handle the pot while painting and decorating without the fear of accidentally denting or breaking it.

The bisque firing also helps the glaze adhere to the clay better when you reach that phase. The temperature for bisque firing will be determined by the type of clay used, but it matters to make sure that your kiln is not too hot. Otherwise, the opposite can cause cracks, especially if your pot has not been dried properly beforehand. It is possible to fire more than one project at once as long as there is enough space for all of them. In the case of plates, for instance, you can stack them on top of each other without any problems.

Underglazing

Underglaze refers to the decorative painting done on the pot. This is where you have the most room to let your imagination run wild. Glazes for this step are numerous and available in hundreds of colors, consistencies, and textures. The techniques vary as well and can be combined for interesting effects. Planning your design is crucial as mistakes are difficult to remove.

Underglazing is also done in layers. To gain the best results, it is important to let one color dry before applying the next on top if you want to avoid unwanted blending or mixing. A good advantage of this is that the designs are baked directly into the clay and covered by a final layer of transparent glaze. This way, the design becomes waterproof and cannot be rubbed off. They form a part of the final product.

For beginners, a simple way to add a glaze to your pot is by dipping it. Dip your pot in the glaze carefully, making sure that all surfaces are covered. Remove your pot and let the excess glaze drip off before setting it down to dry. This technique covers the whole pot quickly and provides a smooth surface.

Dipping can be used in layers for various effects and designs. Another common way to apply a glaze is by using brushes and similar tools. This gives you more control and makes it possible to create intricate designs and images. However, you run the risk of leaving behind visible brush strokes.

Underglazing can be done on both bisque products, as well as raw clay that has been dried. Some types of glazes and other underglaze goods can be more partial towards one or the other. You should always read the instructions and suggestions of every glaze that you use as well.

Bisque or raw clay each have their advantages and disadvantages to be considered when planning. Painting on the latter tends to result in slightly more vibrant colors, and the glazes are absorbed directly into the clay. This is both a blessing and a curse as it is much easier to see where you need to apply a thicker layer to gain a solid color. Still, it is impossible to remove any of the glazes once it has been applied. The raw clay is also fragile and can still be dented, bent, scratched, or damaged when too much force is applied to it. When working with bisque clay, there is a chance that colors may become slightly duller when they are baked into the clay afterward. The color may also end up uneven in certain areas. When painting design, the glaze remains on the surface of the clay, so it is possible to wipe off most of the glaze when you make a mistake. However, it is also easier to smudge your work if you are not careful.

On bisqueware, it is easy to paint various layers over each other, which can be a great way to create interesting textures and effects. But it can be problematic if you are aiming for a perfectly smooth surface. Bisqueware is also firmer than raw clay, and there are many tools like underglaze crayons and pens that will dent the latter but not the former. Some types of glazes can even dissolve raw clay while creating your design.

The final layer of glaze is usually clear, stained, or transparent. It will form a protective coating over the other colors and give the whole pot a more solid, glass-like look. This can sometimes be referred to as a topcoat. If you want your pot to hold liquids, you should glaze the inside of your pot as well.

Glaze Firing

This is the last step in the glazing process. It can only start once your final layer of glaze is dry. Firing the glaze means heating the pot in your kiln until the glaze melts and fuses with your clay. It is also known as bringing the glaze and clay to maturity. The type of glaze and clay will determine the necessary temperature, but the latter must rise and fall slowly to avoid damage to the pot. It is also important for none of your ceramics to touch each other at all when you are firing more than one project at a time. If two of them touch, the glazes will melt into each other and fuse the pots.

Firing the glaze also gives the pot a glass-like look and feel and strengthens it. It is one of the most important phases of ceramic work in which your pot can be ruined in an instant if handled carelessly. Always make sure to follow the instructions for your glaze, clay, and kiln to avoid that.

Once the firing process is complete, let your pot cool to a manageable temperature before taking it out. In some cases, it may be necessary to sand off some sharp corners, but it can be done quickly and easily to add the finishing touches of your pot.

Traditional and Modern Ceramics

As ceramics have developed through the ages, it is only natural to see a significant difference between traditional and modern ceramics, which are also known as advanced or precise ceramics. The materials, techniques, and availability have a large impact on the final result.

The first distinction is the clay itself. Traditional ceramics use a single or mixed type of natural clay. It limits the crafter when it comes to the clay varieties, but they can be inexpensive, especially in areas where natural clay is abundant.

Modern clay, on the other hand, is chemically treated with oxides, minerals, and other inorganic materials to enhance, reduce, or alter specific properties of the clay, such as texture, density, strength, water resistance, etc. This gives you a lot more room to be specific to your work. You can also choose the clay that's best suited to your needs, but more enhanced types of clay can be expensive.

These differences have a further impact on the structure of your work. The raw materials used in traditional clay tend to have many more flaws within a single piece of clay, such as discoloration, irregular texture, and weaknesses. Together with a much more complex chemical construction, it is hard to predict the final product or how much you can control the clay. Although these factors can be huge setbacks, many artists believe that these flaws give the project more character and personality.

Meanwhile, the clay used in modern ceramics is much more uniform and precise. The chemical reaction to firing is perfectly controlled as well. With consistent coloring and texture, the final result can be determined early.

Because of such differences, traditional and modern ceramics have vastly diverse functions. The former is commonly used for household objects, such as plates, or cups or building materials like bricks. The latter has a much wider range of uses because of how easily the clay can be matched to specifications. Modern ceramics have multiple applications that stretch from biological to technological and play a large role in the development of new materials.

When it comes to using ceramics in arts, there is no right or wrong between the two forms. It is up to you as an artist to choose what you prefer.

Chapter 2
Equipment

Equipping your ceramic studio can be difficult and pricey, and you are bound to build up an impressive collection over time. However, there are some things to get you started that you can't go without even as a beginner.

Glazes

First and foremost, you need to apply a glaze to your pot. If you are new to the art, it is best to invest in only a few glazes to test out and experiment with and move onto more expensive and complicated glazes as you progress and grow more experienced. Glazes can also be made, and this book will contain a few recipes later.

Mixing Tools and Containers

Many glazes can be bought in powder form and need to be combined with liquids to activate them. For this, you need a bowl and spoon or whisk. These are easy to find in the kitchen. However, because the chemicals in glazes are often toxic, you should set aside containers, mix implements specifically for this purpose, and set them aside from your cooking implements. You also need containers or tools if you are mixing glazes for new colors. Keeping a few airtight containers, even if they are old coffee jars, empty yogurt containers, or old Tupperware since excess glaze can be used again. In some cases, the glaze powder that you buy may come in a plastic or paper bag, and you need a more suitable container.

Application Tools

There are dozens of tools that can be used to apply a glaze to your ceramic project. However, as a start, a small set of four to six paintbrushes is all you need, ranging from reasonably wide to extremely thin. Those should be enough to help you cover large areas of your pot quickly or paint delicate designs and details. Simple, decent quality paintbrushes are perfectly fine if you do not want to immediately jump into buying specialized glaze brushes right from the start. Sponges can also be used to create interesting textures when applying a glaze and are relatively easy to come by. You can even use an old toothbrush to create a splatter effect.

Another useful application tool for glazes is a plastic bottle with a very thin nozzle--like those commonly used for sauces at food stands.

These small nozzles are great for drawing thin lines, filling up a pace, and creating dripping effects with your glazes. They can also double as an airtight container if you switch out the nozzle for a regular lid.

Basic Stationery

Especially if you are a beginner, you want to draw out your design on your pot with a pencil before applying your underglaze. For this, you need a light pen that's easy to erase, as well as a suitable eraser. Kneadable erasers are usually a better option as they do not leave any rubbings behind on your clay. It is essential to use a soft pencil and work gently when drawing a design onto raw clay that has not been bisqued. A ruler is also a useful tool as you will most likely need precise measurements and straight lines at some point or another. It can be tricky to use on rounded surfaces but can be replaced with a measuring tape.

You may also need a sketch pad or some paper if you want to plan your design first or experiment with ideas. Sturdy paper is an excellent material to use if you are going to make your own stencils.

Turntable

Especially if you are a pottery artist, you should already have a turntable handy. It is a great way to cover your entire pot with glaze and turn it around to paint other areas without actually handling the pot. Meaning, you won't risk leaving fingerprints or smudges in the wet glaze. It will also allow you to paint straight horizontal lines around your pot without your hand wavering or moving out of place.

Your turntable does not need to be a professional or electronic pottery tool. Even a simple turntable or a Lazy Suzan that you turn by hand should be adequate. If you are very handy and diligent, you can also build your own using the necessary materials.

Kiln

The kiln is one of your most essential pieces of equipment when working with ceramics and glazes as it is the only way to fire them accurately. Neither your oven nor an open fire will reach temperatures high enough. There are several styles of the kiln with different designs, sources of heat, and ways of controlling the said heat, from using wood or oil for fuel to being completely electric.

A kiln is an expensive enterprise, however, whether you buy one or build one yourself. Rather than investing in a kiln immediately, you should find nearby pottery or ceramics studio and borrow their kiln for a while until you are confident that you will spend enough time and effort on ceramics to make your kiln worthwhile.

Miscellaneous Tools

Other than your proper glazing tools, there are some odds and ends that all artists need, such as glasses of water to rinse brushes, paper towels, etc. Some tools can help make the glazing process a little easier.

Firstly, you will need an old tablecloth or newspaper to keep your work surface clean if you are working on a table or desk at home. If you have your kiln, you can place thin sheets of dried clay under your work when firing to protect the racks of your kiln. A simple drying rack or cooling is also a good idea so that you have somewhere safe and convenient to dry your glazes before firing or adding a layer to it. You will need old washcloths to wipe glaze off your hands, as well as a filter mask as breathing in the glaze powder can be hazardous. You should also have one or two old plates for mixing small amounts of colors or testing new pigments.

Glaze Recipes

To help you get started, here are a few easy recipes for glazes that you can make at home. The ingredients required can be bought at specialized stores and are reasonably inexpensive. The methods are structured in a percentage format, making it easy to prepare them for different batch sizes. If you are making 100 oz. of glaze powder, and a single ingredient is listed as 25%, for instance, you simply need to use 25 oz. of said ingredient.

Recipe 1 - Matte Dipping Glaze

This recipe requires:

- 42% Flint

- 38% Gerstley Borate

- 10% Lithium Carbonate

- 5% Grolleg Kaolin

- 5% Nepheline Syenite

This powder should be mixed at a ratio of 10-11 oz. of water per 1 lb of glaze powder and fired at cone 6 or low fire. You can add 10% to 15% stains for bright colors.

Recipe 2 - Eggshell Glaze

This recipe requires:

- 44.5% Ferro Frit 3124

- 20% Custer Feldspar

- 9.5% Whiting

- 8% Silica

- 7.5% Bentonite

- 5.5% Zinc Oxide

- 5% EPK Kaolin

Mix the ingredients at a ratio of 6-7 oz. of water per 1 lb of powder for a brushing glaze or 10-11 oz. of water for a dipping glaze. It should be fired at cone 6 or mid-range fire. You can add 9% tin oxide or 3% red iron oxide for color variations.

Recipe 3 - Satin Black Glaze

This recipe requires:

- 20% Flint

- 20% Soda Feldspar

- 20% Custer Feldspar

- 15% Dolomite

- 13% Talc

- 10% Kentucky Ball Clay (OM4)

- 2% Whiting

Mix it at a ratio of 6-7 oz. per pound of powder. This glaze is fired at cone 10 or high fire. You can add 9% red iron oxide and 3% cobalt carbonate for a slightly more brown appearance.

Recipe 4 - Transparent, Glossy Glaze

This recipe requires:

- 46% F-4 Feldspar

- 30% Gillespie Borate

- 13% EPK Kaolin

- 11% Silica

Mix a ratio of 6-7 oz. of water per 1 lb of powder. The glaze is fired at cone 5 or low- to mid-range fire.

Recipe 5 - Semi-Opaque, Semi-Satin Glaze

This glaze requires:

- 44.5% Ferro Frit 3124

- 20% F-4 Feldspar

- 9.5% Whiting

- 8% Silica

- 7.5% Bentonite

- 5.5% Zinc Oxide

- 5% EPK Kaolin

Mix it at a ratio of 6-7 oz. per pound of powder. The glaze is fired at cone 5 or low- to mid-range fire.

Recipe 6 - Opaque, Glossy Glaze

This glaze requires:

- 52.6% Gillespie Borate

- 26.4% Silica

- 21% EPK Kaolin

Mix 6-7 oz. of water with every pound of powder. The glaze is fired at cone 5 or low- to mid-range fire.

Coloring Tips

Recipes 4-6 are colorless, but you can add certain ingredients in amounts of 0.5% - 10% to increase the glazes' pigmentation. This is an excellent chance to experiment a little, but you should always test these glazes before using them as the results will always vary. The colors are only a basic guide, and different ingredients will deliver better or worse products.

Here is a list of ingredients that create specific colors:

- **Blue** - Cobalt Oxide

- **Turquoise** - Copper Carbonate

- **Green** - Chrome Oxide

- **Brown** - Red Iron Oxide

- **Yellow** - Rutile (powder), Yellow Ochre

- **Red** - Manganese Dioxide

Chapter 3
Design and Decoration

Glazes are all about decorating your clay work with beautiful colors and designs, and there are some things you need to know before you jump in. It may be easy to design a repetitive pattern or a more organic design, but there are many options available that can bring your ceramic art to new levels.

Layering

Layering your glazes is an excellent way to bring more depth and dimension as the initial layers can look further away while the newer ones look a little closer. In many cases, especially when working with images and fine details, it is necessary to layer colors on top of each other. In other cases, you may need to add more than one layer to strengthen the intensity of a color. You can further layer different colors thinly over each other to achieve new shades. E.g., put a semi-transparent red glaze over an opaque blue glaze to gain purple. It is also an excellent tool for blending pigments. Piling layers on top of each other or using very thick layers can also help create a three-dimensional effect with your glazes.

Layering Colors

It is essential to know that some colors are more suitable for layering than others. As a general rule, it is better to start with lighter shades and layer the darker ones over them as it is easier to cover the light with dark. This is especially relevant to black and white products. An opaque black glaze will rarely need more than one coat to create a solid color, while an opaque glaze may need several layers to cover up a darker color completely.

Sometimes, the color of your clay may influence the glaze color, making it duller or throwing the shade off. To avoid this, apply a base layer of white first. It also helps when layering a lighter color over another. For instance, when you want to layer red over blue, you can add a white layer under the red to prevent the red from looking a little purple. If your design requires you to layer light colors on top of darker colors, you will need to apply a very thick layer of glaze or several layers of said color. If you do the latter over a large area, you can experiment with different tints and shades of your preferred color underneath two or three layers of the exact hue to bring more dimension and depth into the color.

Yellow is an especially tricky color to work with as it covers darker colors even less effectively than white. It is strongly advised to apply at least one layer of white beneath the yellow, no matter which color you are layering over, if you want a solid yellow. Even with a white base, you will still need to add several coats of yellow glaze for the best results.

Step-by-Step Layering

Step 1: Paint the base color in layers

Make sure that each layer is dehydrated before adding the next layer until you have a solid base.

Step 2: Add the first layer of decorations

We are talking about stripes and spots or textures that will show through all your other designs. Some colors may need more than one layer. Let them dry completely.

Step 3: Put down the base colors

Do it on the first layer of your design. For instance, you can add base colors for the stem and a few leaves if you are painting a flower. You can blend colors at this step if you want. If some elements are meant to look like they are behind others, they should be on the first layer.

Step 4: Add details on top

Once the base colors are dry, add features on top of these colors. For the example above, you can make veins and outlines for your leaves, as well as highlights and drop shadows on your stem.

Step 5: Place base colors for the next layer

Begin placing the base colors for the next layer of design, such as the petals of your flower. Remember to let each coat dry before you add another layer for a more solid color.

Step 6: Add details to the new layer

Add details to this new layer of design, such as the veins and outlines of your flower petals. Keep on repeating the layering process until you are satisfied with your design.

Step 7: Add one or two layers of clear, transparent glaze to your entire work

Doing so will give the layers a sense of unity and make sure that the whole product is covered with a protective glaze. This is an excellent opportunity to make your project glossier or more matte or give everything a particular tint.

Step 8: Place your ceramic in the kiln

Once the last layer is dry, fire the ceramic to seal the glaze.

Specific Gravity

In simple terms, the specific gravity refers to the consistency of the glaze. As an example, if 100 mL of water weighs 100 g, it has a specific gravity of 1. If 100 mL of glaze weighs 140 g, its specific gravity is 1.4. High specific gravity means that the glaze is very thick, while low specific gravity means that the glaze is thin and watery.

Finding out the specific gravity is relatively simple and requires nothing more than a container, a gram scale, and a measuring cup.

To start, weigh the container and write down the weight. Next, fill it with 100 mL of glaze and weigh it again. Subtract the weight of the container to the weight of just the glaze. Divide the result by the volume of glaze to get its specific gravity. If you are working with 200 mL of glaze, divide the weight by 200 mL.

The specific gravity may look like a number to you, but with time and practice, you will be able to tell the specific gravity by looking at the glaze. The specific gravity is a great tool to get the right consistency when mixing powder glaze or your own glazes. An excellent reference to work with is a specific gravity of roughly 1.3 to 1.55 for brushing glazes and a little lower for dipping glazes. If you buy a liquid glaze in a store, though, the label typically shows its specific gravity.

Surface Design

Creating a design for your pot takes some planning and consideration. You should always think of the seven elements of design, namely shape, color, line, mood, texture, space, and balance.

Shape refers to the overall feeling of the forms you want to use in the design. You can decide between round, circular, and angular shapes overall. When it comes to ceramics and pottery, it is essential to contemplate the shape of the item. The type does not necessarily have to match the shape of your bowl, but they should complement each other.

Color is relatively easy to understand, and you should consider the overall look that you have in mind, be it contrasting or matching colors, light or dark, pastel or neon, etc.

The line does not merely refer to stripes but the types of lines that you will utilize, especially if you are imaginative. You can try sharp, hard edges for one design or soft, curving lines in another.

The mood is a crucial element of the design process, which refers to the emotions that you want to evoke. E.g., joy, sorrow, anger, or peace. You need to choose your mood early as it affects all other elements of design.

Texture denotes how the surface feels. To be precise, is it smooth, rough, or porous? The type of clay you use already does much to create a specific texture, but you can still try various glazes and application techniques to create other surfaces.

Space indicates the free expanse that you can put your design on. The entire surface of your pot is your canvas, and you need to use it wisely. The size of your design elements and their placement should be part of the decision-making process. The negative space can have a significant impact on the overall success of your project, too.

Finding balance in your design is critical. No matter what type you use, all the elements must work in unison. Do not overuse one or two of them to exclude others, or neglect a component until it is completely overpowered. Even within a single option, you need to balance it, especially if you are into sharp contrasts.

Graphic Design and Imagery

Graphic design combines illustration, imagery, and written words to communicate with others. This is most commonly used in advertisements but can be a tremendous ceramic tool to portray a clear message to the viewers

Typography is an essential aspect of graphic design. Not only the words themselves help but also their size, color, and font. It is even possible for the words to be completely random or make no sense since their visual element gives them meaning. Even if you use words only as a background for your design, they will carry a certain mood or association with them.

Similarly, you can use graphic design without written words and focus on using imagery to convey your message. In terms of art, representation refers to the use of strong visual elements that invoke specific thoughts and feelings. An excellent example of that is the use of hearts or the color red to portray love and passion, as well as thick, harsh, dark lines to portray aggression or violence. By using the right imagery, you can tell a whole story or evoke strong emotions with your ceramics. By combining different forms, you can develop your story or message and add more layers of emotion to the piece.

Chapter 4
Practical Application

Now that you know how to plan your layers and create your design, it is time to start glazing your ceramic work.

Prepping for a Better Glaze

Preparing your ceramic project before you start glazing is vital as you want to make sure that your working surface is in the best condition. Doing so will allow you to apply your glaze correctly and prevent possible flaws or chipping.

Bisque firing can be a form of preparation. If you have done this technique, it is essential to sand the piece before glazing it lightly. The reason is that the clay may have small lumps or points that may become more prominent once you start the coating process. A slightly rougher and more porous surface will also hold the glaze better once you apply it and absorb the glaze a little quicker. If you are not working with bisqueware, though, you should avoid sanding as it may dent your clay.

Another vital part of the preparation is making sure that your ceramic is clean. If there is any dust or grime, the glaze won't stick to the surface properly. The application can be difficult, especially if dust mixes into your glaze. Any dirt can also cause problems when firing the glaze, such as imperfections, unexpected color variations, or weaknesses. These areas may also chip easier than other areas.

It is especially important to make sure that the base does not have any glaze to prevent it from sticking to your kiln. When working with bisqueware, to be precise, ceramic artists apply a wax to the base to ensure that they won't be able to use glaze on it accidentally.

One of the quickest and easiest ways to make it happen is by using melted candle wax. However, it tends to create smoke and can be a fire hazard when firing. The good thing is that there are various types of specialized waxes available in stores now. But whichever you use, always try not to get any wax where you do not want it. It will resist the glaze, and you may end up ruining your design.

Application Techniques

Here are some of the most common and popular techniques for applying an underglaze.

Paper Resist

Paper resist can almost be considered as a reverse stencil. It works better with greenware than bisqueware.

For starters, draw your design on a piece of paper and cut it out. Place the design on the surface of your pot and pat it with a damp sponge carefully until it sticks. Then, paint a layer or two of underglaze or glaze over the design. Let it dry to the point where touching the glaze won't cause any damage. After that, peel off the paper slowly so that it will not rip or leave behind any residue. The original color of the clay should be visible where the paper has been.

Sgraffito

This is a unique technique that involves carving off a layer of glaze to reveal a different colored glaze underneath. It works best with slips and basic glazes and requires a sgraffito tool that's specifically designed for it.

To perform sgraffito, apply the first color and let it dry thoroughly. Apply the next layer of color, making sure that it is even and forms a solid color. Once the second layer is dry, draw on the area that you want to carve first. After that, carve off the outer layer of glaze.

This technique takes a lot of time and patience as a single mistake can ruin your whole design, and starting over will take a lot of work. It is a good idea to use contrasting colors when you try sgraffito.

Layered Sgraffito

For layered sgraffito, slips work better than glazes and underglazes. After applying the base color, apply several coats of differently colored slips, letting each layer dry. Once the final layer is dehydrated, you can begin drawing your design and carving. Carving deeper or more shallowly will reveal a different segment of color, and the use of broader, more rounded sgraffito tools can reveal several layers at once. This technique often requires subtlety and precision.

Layered sgraffito can also be used to create complex images with various layers, but this calls for a large amount of planning. As with regular sgraffito, apply a coat of color over the base and carve out all the parts of the design that you want in the base color. Once done, fill the carved areas with wax resist carefully and cover it with another layer of colored glaze or slip. Trying not to cut too deeply, carve out more of your design to reveal the second color underneath. Keep on doing this process until you have used all the desired colors.

When firing, the wax resist will melt away, accurately revealing the full design and all the colors for the first time.

Mishima/Inlay

The first step needs to be done when the clay is still wet. After forming your clay into the desired shape, let it dry for a day or two until it becomes as hard as leather. Cover it with a wax resist and air it out some more before cutting your design, removing the resist, and carving the lines directly into the clay. Let the clay dry completely.

Use a brush to apply thick layers of glaze, underglaze, or slips over your pot, making sure to fill the carved lines well. You can even use a different type of clay for this. Once the glaze is dry, bisque your work to harden the glaze and melt off the wax. The excess glaze will be removed with the wax and leave behind your design with the carved lines neatly filled. Now, you can add decorations with underglazes or a clear topcoat and fire your glaze to finish your project.

Slip Trailing

Slip trailing uses slips, a unique mixture of clay, water, and colorants, to create raised lines on the surface. A slip trailer is a tool needed for this technique, and it works by continuously releasing a stream of your slip, similar to piping icing on cakes. You can, however, improvise by using a cond

trailer with the slip and draw your design carefully. Although you can use it on bone-dry iment applicator or piping tool.

Fill your slipclay or bisqueware, it works best with hard, raw clay.

The advantage of slip trailing is that it is perfectly safe to use glazes and underglazes over it. If you bisque fire your work after this technique, the slip will become a part o of your ceramic piece and cannot be rubbed off or scratched easily.

Transfer

In terms of ceramic art, transfer merely refers to transferring an image or design from a piece of paper to the surface of your clay. One of the simplest and more traditional ways of doing a transfer is by using slips and paper. Use colored slips to paint your desired image on the paper in layers, working in reverse.

Start by painting the details that usually appear in the last layer and then fill out the colors and add some background designs before adding the background color. You need to work quickly as you do not want the slips to dry out too soon.

Working with leather-hard clay, place the paper on your ceramic piece, with the slip against the clay. You need to be very careful with your placement. Let the transfer sit on the clay for a few seconds, then use a rib or scraper to press the slip deeper into the clay and smooth out the image. Gently peel the paper to reveal your image and let it dry. You can add an optional clear glaze as a topcoat and proceed to fire your work.

A more modern way of transferring an image is by using transfer glaze, which is designed specifically for this purpose and can be found in most art supply stores. Print the copy on an all-purpose paper using an inkjet printer and make sure to avoid using ink that's designed to prevent bleeding when the paper is wet. Paint a liberal layer of transfer over the glaze, pushing it into the paper as much as possible. Let the glaze dry and do it again around five to ten times, allowing each layer to dry thoroughly before adding the next.

An excellent tip to prevent visible brush strokes is to alternate between horizontal, vertical, and diagonal brush strokes when applying every layer. To be safe, let the glaze dry overnight. Soak the paper with the glaze in room temperature water and carefully rub the paper off. You should end up with a rubbery sheet of clear glaze with the image printed on it. The latter will be semi-transparent, so make sure that your ceramic has a single base color that won't affect the color of your image too severely.

Pat the water off the transfer and place it on your ceramic, ensuring its smoothness and lack of wrinkles or bubbles. Paint a layer of transparent glaze over the transferred image to help stick it to the clay and seal it, and then proceed to fire the glaze. This technique works on both raw clay and bisqueware and can be used over dried layers of slip or underglaze.

Different brands and types of transfer glazes will have specific instructions, and it is always essential to follow them.

Painting

Painting is one of the most common and straightforward ways of putting designs on your ceramics. Whether you are using slips, underglazes, or glazes, a simple paintbrush will work perfectly fine. In terms of creating patterns, filling space with color, blending, or making detailed images, the principles are the same as painting on a regular canvas. The primary difference is that the ceramic work has curves and corners instead of being flat. The consistency of the glaze may also be a little different.

The biggest problem with painting ceramics is the risk of seeing visible brush strokes. It takes time and care to avoid them. Still, painting allows you to add any image and pattern.

This technique works well on leather-hard clay, bone dry clay, or bisqueware, although it is advised to use bisqueware for this as you may develop a habit of resting your hand on the surface while you are painting. If that is the case, you may end up denting the clay unintentionally. Most conventional painting techniques work for painting on ceramics as well.

Maiolica

Maiolica, often referred to as majolica, is a low-fire technique that consists of painting designs onto a white surface. It can be used on leather hard and bone dry clay or bisqueware.

Maiolica uses maiolica glaze, which is tin-based and especially effective in preventing bleeding. To start, cover your work with a matte white maiolica base by dipping it before letting it dry. The consistency of the glaze should be a little thicker than regular dipping glazes. Remove any creases or bubbles and allow the glaze cure for roughly 24 hours.

Once cured, you can draw your design onto the white base with a soft pencil, which will be easy to erase with your fingers if need be. Leaving the background white, paint the foreground elements of your designs using colored maiolica glazes and stain pastes. You can even combine painting with sgraffito for effect.

After that, you can add background elements to the design if you want. Rather than struggling to paint around the foreground elements, cover them with a wax resist and paint on the surface with ease. You can do this in layers until you are satisfied with your design.

It is quite common to leave the background white, but many artists like to change that using the same resist technique. Once your background is done, you can add some final touches with the stain pastes and fire your work at cone 5 or low fire.

Glazing Colors

When selecting the colors for your design, it is always crucial to think about the ceramic material that you are using. After all, it can affect the colors of your glaze in unexpected ways. This is not an exact science, and every glaze, no matter what the color is, can react differently. The only way to truly learn what colors work best with different materials is by trial and error, experimentation, and experience. There are, however, some basic rules to help you get started.

For a wide range of colors to work, especially with transparent and translucent glazes, you want to use white, cream, or light gray clay, which is extremely common in stoneware types. Colors are easy to apply and not affected by the color of the clay, but some lighter shades may be hard to see against the bright background.

Clay with a medium gray or light brown color works well with anything, considering both light and dark colors will be visible. Translucent glazes do not match with these clays, though, because their color may affect the glaze. Even some opaque shades may need several layers to ensure that they do not have a slight grey or brown tinge.

Darker clays with a red or brown hue, such as terracotta, are often used for their vibrant color as their designs leave much of the original color visible. Because of this, it can be challenging to find suitable colors for them.

Black is always a beautiful color to use together with these clays, as well as warm colors like dark brown and yellow, which will need several layers. Slightly lighter browns and most shades of red should be avoided altogether as they won't show against the clay. Still, they can be used as a light tint from time to time. Most color combinations may look a bit odd with these red and brown clays, but some experimentation can help you find something that works. Green may be an excellent place to start since it is a complementary color to red. Translucent colors will be challenging to use with these clays as well.

Very dark clays can be tricky to work with because bright colors will be most visible against the background and need several layers to either cover up the dark or be applied very thickly. As mentioned above, they can be used for more subtle effects. A strong black may be reasonably visible depending on the clay, but transparent and translucent glazes will make almost no difference on their own. Several layers of translucent glazes may be able to change the tint a little, but you will need a very thick application to change the color of the clay or make it look lighter.

Some clays are artificially colored, and the only way to find the best shades is by experimenting. If you are in a bind, a color wheel can be a useful tool to guide your choices, too.

Testing Glazes

Testing each glaze before applying it to your ceramic product is one of the most vital parts of the planning process. The reason is that glazes react differently to various types of clay. The color may not always be what you expect, especially when you make your own glazes. Even the store-bought ones need to be tested for their color and consistency, too, because the same glaze from different brands may still have slight variations in such terms. Even if you have chosen one single brand to stick with, you should test your glaze every time you use it since the batches may have minor flaws or differences. The same idea goes for powder glazes.

Luckily, testing a glaze is easy. Here are some necessary steps that you can follow:

Step 1: Prepare a few test samples of the different types of clay that you want to use

Roll out small amounts of clay into a flat surface and let them dry. Ensure that each sample is labeled accurately. In truth, you may want to write down which samples you have prepared.

There are two things you can do in this step that will help you save time throughout the process: make the clay pieces fairly thin so that they can dry and bake a little quicker. Prepare more than one sample of each clay so that you can quickly test several glazes and techniques at once, too. You may want to build up sections, add texture in the clay, and do some light carving to see how the glaze reacts to those elements.

Step 2: Bisque fire your samples if you want to work with bisqueware in your final piece

Otherwise, you can immediately begin testing your glazes when the samples are either leather-hard or bone-dry.

Step 3: Choose and prepare your glazes

When you are ready to begin testing, choose your glazes and develop them according to the instructions. It will be a lot quicker to mix all your powder glazes in one go and have all your glazes within your reach instead of incorporating and testing them individually. Wear a safety mask, especially when you are working with powders.

Step 4: Test for consistency

The first test is the consistency of your glaze, especially when mixing powder glazes with water. You will be able to tell if a glaze is too thick or thin to some extent just by looking at it.

As a guideline, your glaze should seem to have the same consistency of heavy cream. For a slightly more precise test, you can use the spin test. Stir the glaze a little and remove the tool. The glaze will keep that momentum and continue spinning for a short period. That duration will tell you how thick your glaze is. The glaze will keep turning when it is too thin. If it is too thick, it may not even spin at all. For a dipping glaze, the glaze should continue to turn for 8 to 10 seconds.

Another way to test for consistency is through the drip test. Wearing disposable gloves, dip one finger in your glaze and remove it to see how much of the glaze drips off naturally. The glaze should cover your finger smoothly, and around 4 or 5 drops of glaze should drop from it before it settles. The runny or profusely dripping glaze will mean that it is too thin; little or no dripping means that it is too thick.

If the latter occurs, you can mix in more water, but be careful not to add too much. It is safer to add several small amounts of water while stirring instead of pouring one large number. If your glaze is too thin, you can thicken it by adding more powder or letting it sit for a day or two and skimming off some of the water that will separate and settle on top of the glaze.

Step 5: Test your glazes

Once you have the right consistency, it is time to test your glazes on your clay samples. Your tests will be determined by the application technique that you want to use, such as dipping or brushing.

If you wish to try the former method, the right idea is to dip a large section of the clay sample in a single layer. Drip two-thirds of that section in a second layer and then one-third of it in a third layer. This way, you will be able to compare the layers carefully and decide how many coats you need.

For the brushing technique, you can conduct the test by applying small swatches of the glaze, seeing how the color reacts to the clay and experimenting with the thickness of your layers. You can even take this opportunity to see how different glazes react with each other. For sgraffito, for instance, find out how well the glaze can be carved and which colors will work well as the top and bottom layers. It matters always to mark your glaze swatches accurately and take note of what you observe so that you can use them as a reference later.

A way to save time while testing glazes is by working with one glaze at a time and applying it to all your clay samples before moving onto the next glaze. Since glazes tend to dry quickly, there is a chance that your first swatches will be dry by the time you finish with the last sample, and you can immediately move on to the next layer. The reason why it is so much quicker than testing all your glazes on a single clay sample and then moving on is that you only have to wash your application tool once per glaze thoroughly instead of washing it every time you want to switch over to a new glaze. You also have one glaze directly at hand, and you will be able to keep better track of what you are doing more efficiently. You also won't have to continually open and close the lids of your containers as you work.

Step 6: Fire your glazes

The final test is through firing. Once you have tested all your glazes and are satisfied with the results, you should see how they react to firing at different temperatures.

Ideally, you want several clay samples with different glazes so that you can have a full sample at all temperature zones. Unfortunately, it can be very time-consuming, require a lot of repetition, and use up your resources. To avoid this issue, start by firing the glazes at low temperatures. Let the kiln cool and make notes on which glazes have reacted to it and how. You may want to take a picture of this phase to help with your references.

Next, fire the sample at medium-range temperatures. Once again, record the reactions of the glazes. You should also take note of how the low-fire glazes respond to the higher temperatures. Repeat this process with high fire as well.

You should now have a thorough understanding of how each of your glazes and clay types will react. This will allow you to make your final choice on the materials for your project.

Test Tiles

Test tiles can help you test your glazes and experiment a little while still being productive. Test tiles are small rectangles that can be kept as a permanent sample and are easy to store and organize. They are quick to make and can even be sold online. Test tiles for each test glazes differ in terms of ideal thickness, combinations in layering, and their reactions to the clay and kiln.

There are many ways to form your clay into test tiles, from throwing it to rolling it out and cutting the clay into rectangles. Your preferred method does not matter as long as all of the pieces are uniform and labeled or numbered correctly. Having identical tiles makes it easier to compare the results of the glazes themselves.

For the best results, you should add some carving and decorative work to the front of the clay to see how the glaze will react to that. It is also essential to find a way to display the tiles, be it a small hole to hang them by rope, a lip at the foot of the tile, or a little support piece at the back. Once they are formed, let the tiles dry, and bisque fire them if you want; otherwise, continue to test your glazes.

Ideally, you cover a single tile with a glaze, making sure that the labels or numbers match. The glaze is typically applied to the test tile through dipping as that is the quickest and easiest way to get a smooth, uniform surface. Nevertheless, you can try other simple methods like brushing if that's what you prefer.

Once you have covered the tiles with two or three layers of glaze and the glaze has dried properly, fire the tiles according to its specifications. When the kiln is cool, your test tiles are done, and they are ready to be displayed, stored, or sold. Some artists like to create small test cups or bowls instead of tiles, but these often take a little longer to make and consume a lot of space, thus making the storage aspect challenging.

As mentioned before, test tiles can be marketed, but that can sometimes be a challenging, intimidating venture, especially if you are not a natural businessman. Most artists decide to sell some of their test tiles in hopes of earning a little extra when customers are reluctant to buy more significant works. In many cases, the test tiles are sold as decorative ornaments or gifts, and this can be used to your advantage.

A good idea to help you sell your test tiles is to play with their shapes and texture to make them more appealing to the customers. You can even use the holidays for this by selling star-shaped test tiles as Christmas ornaments or heart-shaped tiles as gifts for Valentine's day. You can also sell them as souvenirs by adding your signature or studio logo to every piece. Many artists shape their test tiles to serve a function, such as a small cup, plate, bird feeder, or even just a fridge magnet. A little creativity can bring you far, even with only test tiles.

An essential aspect of selling test tiles that's sometimes overlooked is their display. A beautiful, colorful array of test tiles can help catch a potential client's attention. If you create your glaze recipes and selling them, a test tile showing the said glaze can allow you to gain the consumers' trust.

When selling your test tiles, it will also help not to be greedy. Although you should still cover your losses and make a profit, people will be more willing to buy your goods if they are priced reasonably. A lot of thought often goes into buying ceramic works, and customers may be willing to spend a lot of money on an exquisite work of art. However, for a small decoration purchased in the spur of the moment, which is the most common case with test tiles, a lower price will be more attractive and doable.

Once you have covered all these bases, selling test tiles can be much easier and even become a profitable venture.

Chapter 5
Kilns & Firing

Firing is the final phase of the glazing process that needs to be handled with caution, considering a single mistake can ruin all your work.

Firing Techniques

Just as there are different ways to apply your glazes, there are various techniques to fire them. Here are some ways that have an interesting effect on the final result of your work.

Wood Firing

As the name implies, this technique requires you to utilize burning wood as a source of heat. Wood can build extremely high temperatures, especially inside an enclosed kiln, and is suitable for firing at various temperatures. The temperature and length of the firing process are determined by the type, thickness, and amount of wood you use.

For wood firing, it is necessary to build an intense fire inside your kiln's firebox, with your pots carefully stacked on your racks. The kiln must keep most of the heat inside while still allowing air to the flame. If you want the fire to grow hotter, the simplest way is to give the fire more oxygen through the use of a fan or a blower, which many wood firing kilns have already built-in. Keep adding more wood to the fire to keep it burning longer.

To slowly lower the temperature at the end of the process, stop adding oxygen and fuel. The fire will eventually die out, and the coals will cool after a while. To keep the coals from smoldering too long, you should open the kiln a little to let the hot air escape.

One of the most prominent characteristics of wood firing is the ash from the fire that often reacts to the glaze, creating compelling new patterns and effects. This is often sought after and considered to make any ceramic more unique and valuable. There are many wood firing kilns on the market, but with enough ingenuity and knowledge, it is possible to build your own.

The big problem with wood firing is that it can be a high fire hazard if not treated carefully, and there are a lot of safety procedures to follow. Another problem is that the wood can often be costly.

Salt and Soda Firing

These are two very similar techniques that require a fuel-burning kiln and are not generally suited for an electric kiln.

Salt firing is done simply by adding salt to the fuel used for the fire and often effective with unglazed clay. It can, however, be used with slips and underglazes for some interesting effects. When the salt is exposed to very high temperatures, it creates a chemical that reacts with the chemicals inside the clay to form a liquid glass, building a natural glaze around the pot. Clay fired with salt develops an orange color, and at some point, the vapors will begin running down the side of the clay to create a very distinctive effect associated with salt firing.

To accurately fire with salt, you need to add it to the firebox when the kiln reaches the right temperature to start melting the silica in the clay. You should work carefully when adding the salt. It also matters to use a steel angle and add the salt slowly to give it a chance to combust before it reaches the floor of your firebox. The amount of salt will determine the effect it has on your pot, and it takes practice and experimentation to master this aspect of the technique. All your works should be bisque fired before starting the process of salt firing. Some of the vapors created by salt firing can be toxic, so you should always wear a mask when you do it.

Meanwhile, soda firing uses the same method as salt firing but makes use of soda instead of salt. The results are also very similar, but the most significant difference is that soda is less toxic than salt when it burns, making it a safer material to work with. It is also possible to mix the soda with a few other chemical powders to create new colors and effects.

Raku Firing

This is a very unique and unpredictable technique that involves removing the ceramic from the kiln while the clay is still red hot. The clay is then covered in easily flammable materials, such as newspaper or sawdust, to deprive the work of as much oxygen. It causes different reactions in the glaze and clay, so new colors and effects appear. The clay is then rapidly cooled through exposure to air or water to enhance the results.

Traditionally, the pots go inside a cold kiln that's heated up very quickly. The whole firing process can only take as little as 15 minutes, which extremely short compared to other techniques that take up to 10 hours. It works well with most types of glaze and underglaze. If used on the latter, the clay will absorb most of the oxygen, usually resulting in a beautiful matte black surface.

Raku firing is another technique that requires caution as the hot clay can be a fire hazard. Like with others, you should always wear fire safety gear and use long steel tongs to handle the clay. While it can create wonderful work, it can also cause instability in the clay and flaking, so it is best suited for decorative work.

Crystalline Glazes

These are a particular type of glaze designed to form visible, colored crystals within the glaze when firing. The glaze looks plain, and the crystals are invisible during the application. However, during the firing, the crystals create beautiful effects on the surface of your pot and have a very spontaneous feel. These crystalline glazes are fairly thin and fluid, but they have to be to let the right molecules move around and let the crystals grow. Although the exact placement of these crystals cannot be controlled, you can have a hand in the size and shape of the crystals that form.

Firing is a very significant aspect of crystalline glazes, as this is what allows the crystals to form. The glaze needs to be molten for a long time to give the crystals time to grow. The longer the high temperatures are maintained, the larger the crystals are. The shape can be influenced by the temperature range used for firing. Around 1850-1995°F, it will form round crystals, 2012°F usually causes a double ax-head type shape, and roughly 2084°F will form long, spire type crystals. These are rough estimates, so you should always consult the instructions of each specific glaze for the best firing schedule.

Low to High Fire

Because of the different chemical components in glazes, they need to be fired at different temperatures. If the temperature is too low, the glaze won't reach its melting point and mature. If the temperature is too high, the glaze will melt too much and start to run. That is why different glazes are usually referred to as low fire, mid-range, and high fire glazes.

Low fire refers to a kiln temperature of about 1623-2048°F or cone 012 to cone 02. Although it often results in weaker glazes, raw colors, and porous clay, this is the most traditional range for firing. It allows potters to use colorants that burn or melt away at higher temperatures.

Mid-range is the temperature range between 2167 - 2264°F or cone 4 to cone 7. This range has become more and more popular in recent times, especially with the electric kiln. It is fairly low in fuel consumption and still has a large range of colored glazes that can be used with these temperatures. A big advantage of using this range is that it allows you to work with stoneware clays that do not fully cure in low fire.

High fire ranges between 2305-2530°F or cone 8 to cone 14. Although this temperature leaves you with a minimal range of available colors, it results in the densest and most durable glazes and clay bodies possible. It is mostly used for stoneware and porcelain.

With store-bought glazes, the packaging will usually give you instructions regarding the appropriate firing range, but it can be difficult to figure it out when making your own glazes. Recipes for homemade glazes often provide a firing range as well; through understanding how these recipes work and how to put ingredients together to create your own, you will eventually realize which firing range to use as well.

Oxidation & Reduction

These two terms refer to the acts of adding or removing oxygen during the firing process, respectively. A kiln has enough energy to keep the fuel burning, but nothing more.

During oxidation, excess oxygen is added to the kiln to cause reactions within the clay and glaze to affect their properties. For instance, copper carbonate becomes copper oxide, which can change the color, texture, and density of the clay. The reduction process involves removing oxygen to force the fire to create carbon, which reacts to the compounds in the clay and glaze differently to cause changes in color and texture.

Oxidation and reduction are often used together with the high fire temperature range to create a broader range of available colors.

Most electric kilns have a neutral or slightly oxidized atmosphere and can easily be programmed. Using these techniques with a fuel, burning kiln takes a little more work. It is easy to add oxygen with the use of a fan or blower, but removing oxygen can be difficult and often requires specialized equipment. The reduction process also needs good timing as beginning it too soon or extending it for an extended period can cause instabilities and flaws in your work.

Electric Kilns

Although not as traditional, the electric kiln is a commonly used type of kiln that is generally smaller, neater, easier to clean, and much cheaper to maintain in terms of fuel cost. They are also manageable and can give you precise control over the entire firing process with the touch of a few buttons.

An electric kiln is especially helpful as you can ensure that heating up or cooling down the fire is always slow enough to prevent any bursts of heat from affecting the clay. Electric kilns can be heated and cooled manually by monitoring and managing the cones or an electronic controller that does everything for you. All kilns come with a set of pre-made programs to use for the latter. Made by professionals, it is a great tool to use when you are still getting used to your kiln or creating your own program for something that your kiln may not be able to do with any of its original features.

Although electric kilns come with instructions, they can be a little confusing and complicated to use, especially if you want to follow your own firing schedule rather than a pre-programmed one. So, here are some necessary steps on how to program your electric kiln:

Step 1: Select your program type

There are various types of programs, of which the Ramp and Hold program is the simplest one and will be used for these instructions. It works by completing a programmed action, holding it for as long as needed, and then moving on to the next activity.

Step 2: Indicate how many actions you want the kiln to complete

This will be determined by how many different phases you wish to use for this specific firing session.

Step 3: Select the temperatures for each action

The function of each action is to either heat or cool the kiln to a specific temperature, and the temperature of the previous action determines it. The more actions you choose, the more control you have over the entire process. As an example, you have four actions. The first one is set to heat the kiln to 300°F, the second to heat to 1000°F, the third to heat to 2000°F, and the fourth to cool down back to 300°F before shutting down. The kiln can be set to work with either Fahrenheit or Celsius.

Step 4: Choose the speed at which the action is completed

The rate is usually indicated at Fahrenheit per hour, showing how much the temperature rises every hour.

For instance, you have set the kiln to raise the temperature to 300°F at 150 F/hr. It will take two hours to complete this action. This combination of temperature and time requires a little understanding of heat work, which most of us are familiar with through cooking. It is important to keep these rates practical as it is impossible to jump from 300°F to 1000°F in 5 minutes, and your cool downtime is even more restricted due to heat buildup.

Step 5: Select how long the program should hold each action

If you have a holding time programmed, the kiln will not immediately cross over to the next action as soon as it reaches the programmed temperature. However, it will hold that temperature for as long as you have programmed it to hold.

As an example, the kiln raises the temperature from 300°F to 1000°F at a rate of 200 F/hr, holds the temperature at 1000°F for 30 minutes, begins to heat it up to 2000°F at 250 F/h, and holds that temperature for 3 hours before cooling it back to 300°F at a rate of 400 F/h.

Step 6: Always double and triple check your program

Make sure that you do not have any mistakes everywhere, considering even the smallest typo can cause big problems in your firing process. Once you are sure that your program will do exactly what you want, and your ceramic works are loaded, you can start the program and let it run its course.

Gas Kiln

The gas kiln is one of the more common and efficient fuel-burning types. It is also the most popular kiln for reduction firing, which can be done in a few simple steps.

Step 1: Begin heating your kiln as you would for a regular firing session

Make sure that the kiln is well-ventilated and that you have fair oxygen flow.

Step 2: Start reduction accordingly

The first time you implement reduction in the firing process should happen shortly before your kiln reaches top temperature. With a gas kiln, you will likely be working with cones, so you have to start when the second to last cone begins to tip.

There are several ways to implement reduction according to your kiln. With smaller kilns, for instance, you can use fiber brick or blanket to plug the fire port. For larger kilns, you can partially close the damper on the chimney or the exit hole opening to build pressure. You further have to limit airflow into the kiln by closing the vents a little more, reducing the oxygen flow to your burners, and slowing down your blowers. Make sure that you have just enough air for the burners to keep burning and nothing more.

A telltale sign that your kiln is in the reduction process is the long yellow flames that out of the vents and peepholes of your kiln. You should always steer clear of the peepholes while the kiln is in reduction as it can be dangerous.

Step 3: Let your kiln reach the right temperature

Give your clay and glaze enough time to mature and fully bake while in this phase.

Step 4: Shut down the burner

Once your works have spent enough time in reduction, it is time to shut off your burner. You then close all the vents and fire ports, turn off the blowers, and use fiber brick or fabric to plug up all the peepholes. It is alright if your kiln is not entirely airtight as long as you stop the airflow inside the kiln. Keep it in this state as it cools down naturally.

Chapter 6
Reglazing

The biggest mistake that new ceramic artists make is thinking that reglazing is a quick process that can fix flaws or unwanted effects in a snap. Reglazing takes a lot of time, and many feel like it is easier to make a new piece from scratch. Still, there may be just one small mistake or problem in an otherwise perfect glaze, and a little bit of effort on a reglaze can save the piece.

One of them is that you are not working on bisqueware or clay anymore. The glazed surface is not porous enough to let the new glaze adhere properly, but there are several ways to improve your chances. Many use adhesives such as hair spray, spray starch, or white glue to cover the piece and reglaze once it is dry. Other artists prefer to add adhesive materials like bentonite, CMC Gum, or detergent to the glaze. The instructions for reglazing use the more traditional method of reheating the piece to slightly soften the old glaze and make it more willing to absorb the new glaze.

Step 1: Reheat the piece

This can be done in the oven, microwave, kiln, or with a heat gun. Reheating does not require nearly as much heat as firing, but you should still use pliers or tongs to handle the piece since it can burn your skin.

Step 2: Apply a thin layer of glaze

Using your preferred application method, apply a thin layer of glaze to the piece, and let it dry. You will need to work quickly while the piece is still hot; otherwise, you may have to reheat it with a heat gun.

Step 3: Add another layer or two of glaze if needed

If not, you can fire your work in the kiln again using the minimum temperatures necessary for the glaze to mature. Let the kiln cool down before handing the piece.

When reglazing, two significant mistakes occur quite often. The first mistake is refiring the piece too much. Firing pieces repeatedly will make the clay and glazes brittle. There is a limit to how much you can refire a piece before it becomes too fragile.

The second mistake is that new layers of glaze are applied too thickly. If the new glaze is too thick, there won't be any opportunity for oxidation between the old and new glaze, and the glaze won't adhere to the piece.

Chapter 7
Common Glazing Problems & Tips

In this chapter, you will see solutions to general problems that may occur during your glazing process, as well as some tips to make the glazing process a little easier.

5 Common Glazing Problems

Crazing

Crazing happens when your glaze forms fine, hairline cracks after going through the firing process. This occurs when the glaze expands more than the clay and has to further contract during the cooling process. There are several causes for this, but the two most common ones include the glaze having been applied too thickly and the pot cooling too quickly after firing. It can also be due to a lack of chemicals like silica and zinc oxide or overuse of alkali. There is not much you can do to fix crazing when it has happened, but you can take steps to prevent it from happening again.

For instance, you can apply the layers of glaze more thinly, as well as increase your firing temperature. Let the work fire longer at maximum temperature and cool down at a much slower rate. You can also add silica and boron to the glaze if that is your problem or replace some of your alkali-based ingredients if you are making your recipe.

Crazing can also take place when the clay absorbs moisture and expands over time. The best solution is to increase your bisque firing temperature or add carbon, zinc, or talc to the clay.

Shivering

Shivering occurs when particles of glaze fall off the clay days or even weeks later. The reason is that the clay expands more than the glaze during firing, compressing the glaze too much. Usually, shivering is the result of too much silica or boron or too little alkali in the glaze. Just like crazing, shivering cannot be fixed but is preventable by reducing the amount of silica, zinc, boron, or quartz in the glaze or clay or adding more soda and potash to the glaze. Sharp edges are especially susceptible to shivering.

Crawling

Crawling happens when the glaze leaves areas of clay completely uncovered or does not adhere to the clay properly, especially during firing. A simple can be the oily or dusty marks on the bisqueware before the application. It can also be the result of oxides like chrome and rutile in underglazes that prevent the glaze from sticking. You can add borax, frit, or clay to the glaze to avoid this.

High-surface tension during firing or when the glaze melts can also cause crawling. The best way to prevent this is by replacing them with more suitable ingredients if you are mixing your glaze.

Lime Popping

Lime popping usually occurs a few weeks or months after glazing when small pieces of limestone or plaster expand after absorbing moisture and forge the glaze off the clay. Other problems look similar to this, but an excellent way to identify it is by looking for small white particles of limestone or plaster embedded in the flakes. This is the result of contaminated clay and an especially common problem with recycled clay.

Storing your clay correctly and taking care when mixing and preparing your clay is the best way to prevent this. If your clay is already contaminated with limestone, you can fish out the contaminants or screen the clay through a fine mesh. However, plaster is nearly impossible to remove from the clay, especially if it is still in powder form. The only thing you can do is to throw out the contaminated clay.

Cracking

The main reason why a glaze can crack when it is drying or in the early phases of the firing process is that it shrinks too much. This excessive shrinking is the result of too much plastic material, such as ball clay, in the glaze. The problem can be the recipe itself or over-grinding, which happens when the particles in your glaze are broken down and made more plastic by being mixed with drill mixers too long and often.

The solution is to replace ball clay with kaolin in the recipe, add CMC Gum to the glaze, and remove bentonite. It will also help to manage your glaze consistency and application, considering thick glazes are more likely to crack than the thinner ones.

12 Helpful Tips

1. The color of a glaze is usually different after glazing than when you apply it because of how the chemicals react to the firing process. To make sure that your final result is exactly what you want, you should always read the instructions carefully and consult your test tiles.

2. Especially when working with figurines or complicated shapes, you should finish all the nooks and crannies first. You are likely to make contact with other areas on your clay surface when trying to reach them, which will cause smudging and fingerprints if they are already glazed and ruin your work. You will also have more peace of mind and be more relaxed while painting the rest of your work, knowing that the most difficult parts are done.

3. An essential element of the design is contrast, especially when it comes to particular areas. Because details are usually fine, thin lines often lose their effect when the background color is too similar to the color of the details. So, make sure to use strong contrasts, such as light and dark colors, to keep your work visible. A good way to find variation is by using

complementary colors, which are on the opposite side of the color wheel.

4. A big problem with brushing on a glaze is that you risk leaving brush strokes behind. To avoid that, use a brush with soft bristles, which flow better over the surface of your clay and make less prominent marks and lines than hard brushes.

5. Even with a soft brush, preventing brush strokes in a single layer is nearly impossible. Despite that, adding at least two extra layers of glaze will help cover the brush strokes. You can also change the direction of your brush strokes for every layer to disguise them.

6. The oil on your skin that often remains on the clay when handling bisqueware can be problematic as it may prevent the glaze from sticking to the surface. Even if you make an effort to clean your hands and bisqueware, the issue may still exist unless you wear disposable gloves. After all, you are bound to get your hands covered in glaze, and you do not want to ruin your best pair of gloves.

7. Always clean your bisqueware after firing. Bisque firing can produce a large amount of bisque dust, which is just as bad for glaze

adhesion as regular dust.

8. The best way to mix your glazes is by stirring instead of shaking them. Doing the latter in a sealed container may seem like a faster and easier method, but you run the risk of letting the lid slip or dropping the container and covering yourself, your workspace, and your clay with glaze.

9. Before you start glazing, always make sure to clean your kiln, even if it has remained closed since the last use. The kiln can gather a surprising amount of dust that can stick to your glazes. You can use a duster or a vacuum cleaner to clean the inside of your kiln, the shelves, and the lid quickly.

10. Whenever you begin glazing, you should avoid taking glaze directly out of your large container. No matter how carefully you work, dust or residue from a different glaze may still get stuck to your brush, which can potentially ruin your whole batch. It is more ideal for scooping small amounts of glaze into a smaller vessel or onto a pallet or lid.

11. With older liquid glazes, you will inevitably find dried glaze around the edges of your container. These flakes may cause some unwanted texture if you accidentally brush

them onto your clay. To prevent this, sieve the glaze through a fine mesh and transfer it to a clean container.

12. Whether it is a small room in your house or a professional studio, make sure that your workspace is comfortable and practical according to what works for you. People often underestimate how much a convenient station can improve this creative process. You can open or close the curtains if you feel like it, arrange your glazes and tools in any way you prefer, and play your favorite glazing music. You should always keep a bottle of water and a snack handy for those days when you get lost in your work as well.

Conclusion

As you can see, glazing is a wonderful way of expressing your creativity and creating exceptional works of art using ceramics. It is understandably not the easiest thing to do in the world. It is not the most glamorous activity either, considering you must deal with adhesives, paints, etc. Not to mention, you need to play with fire (quite literally) to make sure that the glaze will stick.

Is glazing doable for beginners, though?

Absolutely!

This was the reason why I decided to write this book. I wanted to help newbies such as yourself to learn how to create glazes and apply them to a ceramic product. Not only will it protect the latter, but it will also make its beauty last. Won't it be amazing to create a vase, plate, or pot that your future children or grandchildren can inherit?

I hope this book has helped you understand the basics of glazing better and improve the quality of your work. Thank you for buying this book, and I wish you happy glazing sessions for the foreseeable future.

References

Durig, N. (2019, August 23). *Wood Kiln Firing Techniques and Tips*. Retrieved from Ceramic Arts Network: https://ceramicartsnetwork.org/daily/clay-tools/ceramic-kilns/wood-kiln-firing-techniques-and-tips/

Frenzel, H. (2019, April 17). *How to Fire A Gas Kiln Efficiently*. Retrieved from Ceramic Arts Network: https://ceramicartsnetwork.org/daily/clay-tools/ceramic-kilns/fire-gas-kiln-efficiently/

Gardner, R., & Isenstein, B. (2017, August 14). *Creating the Layered Look with Commercial Glazes and Underglazes*. Retrieved from Ceramic Arts Network: https://ceramicartsnetwork.org/daily/ceramic-supplies/ceramic-glazes-and-underglazes/creating-the-layered-look-with-commercial-glazes-and-underglazes/

KILNARTS.ORG. (2019). *Kilns 101*. Retrieved from KILNARTS.ORG: https://kilnarts.org/education/kilns-101/operating/programming/

Montanes, C. (2019, January 18). *Precise Ceramics VS Traditional Ceramics*. Retrieved from Advanced Ceramic Materials: https://www.preciseceramic.com/blog/precise-ceramics-vs-traditional-ceramics/

Munn, J. (2019, May 27). *Slip Trailing for Beginners: A Primer on a Great Ceramics Decorating Technique*. Retrieved from Ceramic Arts Network: https://ceramicartsnetwork.org/daily/pottery-making-techniques/ceramic-decorating-techniques/slip-trailing-for-beginners/

Norsker, H., & Danisch, J. (1993). *Glazes - for the Self-Reliant Potter*. Eschborn: Deutsche Gesellschaft für Technische Zusammenarbeit (GTZ) GmbH.

Northern Beaches Ceramics. (2013, June 6). *To Wax Or Not To Wax*. Retrieved from Northern Beaches Ceramics: https://northernbeachesceramics.wordpress.com/2013/06/06/to-wax-or-not-to-wax/

Peterson, B. (2018, June 12). *Governing Oxidation and Reduction Atmospheres When Firing Pottery*. Retrieved from The Spruce Crafts: https://www.thesprucecrafts.com/oxidation-and-reduction-atmospheres-2745940

Peterson, B. (2019, June 10). *How to Underglaze Pottery*. Retrieved from The Spruce Crafts: https://www.thesprucecrafts.com/when-to-underglaze-pottery-2746192

Peterson, B. (2019, September 2). *The Firing Process for Making Ceramics*. Retrieved from The Spruce Crafts: https://www.thesprucecrafts.com/an-overview-of-the-firing-process-2746250

Peterson, B. (2019, June 30). *Understanding Crystalline Glazes in Pottery*. Retrieved from The Spruce Crafts: https://www.thesprucecrafts.com/what-are-crystalline-glazes-2745879

Peterson, B. (2019, October 17). *Retrieved from Temperature Ranges for Firing Glazes*. Retrieved from The Spruce Crafts: https://www.thesprucecrafts.com/temperature-ranges-for-firing-glazes-2746233

Pottery Making Info. (2019). *Pottery Making: An Introduction*. Retrieved from Pottery Making Info: https://www.potterymakinginfo.com/pottery-making/

Pugel, D. (n.d.). *How to Measure Specific Gravity*. Retrieved from AMACO.com: https://www.amaco.com/clay_how_tos/207

Schukei, A. (2018). *6 Different Ways to Use Underglazes with Ceramics*. Retrieved from The Art of Education University: https://theartofeducation.edu/2018/05/21/6-different-ways-to-use-underglazes-with-ceramics/

The Ceramic School. (n.d.). *How to Mishima a Mug*. Retrieved from The Ceramic School: https://ceramic.school/how-to-mishima-a-mug/

The Ceramic School. (n.d.). *How to Sgraffito*. Retrieved from The Ceramic School: https://ceramic.school/how-to-sgraffito/

Intermediate Guide to Ceramic Glazing

Introduction

In this book, I will delve a little deeper into the art, looking at slightly more complex techniques and concepts, and going into deeper details on other subjects. The purpose of this book is to bring your ceramic art to new heights and ascend beyond the classification of a beginner.

I've put a lot of effort into making this book as simple and easy to understand in the hopes of making ceramics feel more fun. I know very well how tedious it can be to read through pages and pages of complex explanations and descriptions that teach me barely anything that I can apply practically. Still, sometimes explanations of how something works are necessary. In those cases, I've done my best to sum them up into only the most important facts and to keep the terms as simple and straightforward as possible.

Still, you don't need to be a master of the arts with years of experience before you use this book. As long as you've got a good understanding of the basics of pottery glazing and enough knowledge to tell the difference between bisqueware and greenware, you have enough experience to use this book to its full potential.

Chapter 1

Before You Start

The most important thing to do before starting a ceramics project is to plan. No matter how great your skills are, or how much experience you have, if you don't plan, you won't be able to get the best out of your work. You can never do enough planning, and even if you end up doing something that wasn't part of your planning, your planning will still have helped you get a better idea of what you wanted.

The first step of your planning is deciding what you want to do. Whether you're making a pot, bowl, tea set, or decorative sculpture will affect every aspect of your planning, such as your clay, technique, time management, and the type of design you want to work with. Once you've decided on what you're making, you can go on to plan when you're going to create your work, making sure you have enough time scheduled for each phase of the process.

Once you've decided what you want to make, you need to choose your method and your clay type. This is a very important part of the planning, as certain types of clay work better with different methods, and the clay type may have an influence on your glaze as well. At the end of this chapter, I will give you more information on the properties of different clays and glazes to help you with this.

You now have two choices. You can either immediately plan your glaze, or you can make the piece and plan the glaze while you're waiting for the clay to dry. The advantage of planning your glaze before starting with the clay is that you'll have a better idea of the final product throughout the whole process, and it may be easier to work towards that final goal. On the other hand, having the physical piece in front of you may help you better visualize how your glaze will look on the specific shape, and as it often happens, a piece may not end up in the exact shape you originally planned; you might prefer to create a design to match your final shape, rather than adapting the one you've already made. However, both options are fine, and it's up to you to see which works best for you.

Regardless of when you're planning the glaze, the basic process is the same, and once again choosing what you want. Do you want a solid color, randomly mixed colors, patterns, or a detailed image? These questions are important, as they will determine the type of glazes and application techniques you'll use. For a single color or a gradient from light to dark, a dip might be better. For a simple, repetitive pattern, you may want to consider a stencil or reverse stencil, and for a more detailed piece, painting maybe your best option. Once you've made up your mind on the type of design, application technique, and glaze type, it's time to choose your basic color schemes. It's ok if you don't know the exact shades and colors you want to use, as long as you have a vague idea of the color types, such as light blues for a calm, cool feeling piece, greens and browns for nature-inspired works, reds and yellows for something fiery and exciting, or bright, contrasting colors for a dramatic piece. You can refine your color palette as you go on, and you may want to experiment a little with your colors on test tiles.

Once you have an idea of your color scheme, you should choose your base color to form the background. Then it's just a matter of playing around a little. Draw out your ideas for designs on a piece of paper, using pencils. You also don't need to come up with a complete design all at once. Play around with different ideas, line types, etc. and see what you like. You can also play around with different colored pencils to see which colors you like. You also don't need a perfect, complete design. You may be the type of person who likes to go with their instincts and work without a definite plan. In those cases, having a very basic design or mood board can help you guide your thoughts in the right direction when the time comes. Many artists have their own design process, as should you. Designing the look you want for your glaze should be centered on your own creative processes.

Designing your glaze for layering can be a little more time consuming and complicated, as you will have to put effort into planning every layer, but it can save you a lot of effort in the long run and can help you prevent mistakes. One of the most effective ways to plan for layering is to draw out the final design you want, then analyze it and divide it into separate layers. You may want to draw out each layer to make sure you know what you're doing when it's time to apply your glazes.

Something else to keep in mind is that glazes can be opaque or translucent, thick or thin, textured or smooth, shiny or matte, and they may affect each other when applying in layers. As a part of your planning, you should test out the glazes you want to use. The best way to do this is through test tiles. You can also use this as an opportunity to experiment with mixing colors and getting different effects through layering. This way, you'll know exactly what to expect from your glazes.

Another element to look carefully at when planning is deciding which areas to wax. A big mistake many beginners make is to not wax their bisqueware before glazing. This is vital, as your bisqueware will be fused to your kiln. Always wax any surface of your bisqueware that will be in contact with your kiln and make sure it's clear of any glaze. A fused glaze won't only ruin your bisqueware, but it can also damage your kiln.

Once you're happy with the design and satisfied that you've done enough planning, you can get started on your next masterpiece.

Clay and Glaze Properties

The properties of the glazes and clays you use have a significant influence on the whole process of creating your ceramic work, so it's important to make sure you understand at least the basics.

The main element that separates clay from regular sand or mud is its plasticity. This term refers to the clay's ability to form a solid mass and maintain its shape when wetted with the right amount of water. The clay will not lose its shape once it dries or is baked. The plasticity, as well as the amount of water needed to achieve it, is a big part of how clay is classified into different types. The level of plasticity also has an influence on the final result of your work once it is bisqued and fired. Another unique quality of ceramic clay is that certain components within the clay melt, fuse, and solidify, forming a hard, glass-like quality we want in our ceramics. The temperature at which the clay needs to be fired to meet these components is also an important factor in classifying clay types.

There are three types of clay commonly used called earthenware clays, stoneware clays, and ball clays, which are very easy to come by in stores in both dry and moist form. Two other types that are slightly rarer but still popular are fire clays and kaolin clays.

Earthenware

Earthenware is the most common type of clay, as well as the easiest to work with, making it great for beginners or for experimenting with new techniques. It's the best clay to work with when using the potter's wheel or RAM press. Earthenware clays contain components that melt at fairly low temperatures, meaning they need to be fired at low or mid-range temperatures. They also come in various shades of brown, red, and yellow. The biggest problem with these earthenware clays is that they are fairly brittle, and the baked pieces break fairly easily compared to other clay types. As such, the clay is usually applied fairly thickly. Another problem is that earthenware pieces are also very porous and need to be glazed specifically for waterproofing.

Stoneware

Stoneware clays tend to be a bit less plastic, but are still great to work with. This is also a clay suitable for those less experienced, though not as great as earthenware. True to the name, stoneware tends to vary between white, various shades of grey, and sometimes brown. Different firing methods can be used to alter the colors of the fired piece. Fired stoneware is extremely hard and smooth, but needs to be fired at high temperatures. Stoneware also isn't porous, so you won't necessarily need to glaze it specifically to waterproof it. Stoneware clays are also very popular when it comes to industrial pottery work.

Ball Clay

Ball clay is extremely plastic, contains almost no impurities, and is fired at high temperatures. It usually has a very lovely white, buff or light grey color, which makes it very popular, and produces a very smooth surface.

Although ball clay is very easy to shape and work with, it does shrink quite a lot when firing. If you don't take that into account when shaping your piece, it may ruin weeks of hard work. Because of the excessive shrinking, ball clay is often added to other clays, such as stoneware, to make it more plastic and easier to work with, rather than using pure ball clay.

Fire Clay

Different types of fire clay tend to vary greatly in their general properties, but this type of clay is best known for the extremely high temperature at which it's fired. Fire clay varies in color as well, but usually has black spots caused by iron fragments in the clay. This is often considered to be a very great visual feature. Fire clay is often added to other clays to increase their maximum firing temperature, or to smooth clays, such as stoneware, to give them a rougher texture. Fire clay is also often used to make cones that are used in a fuel kiln to help determine the temperature.

Kaolin Clay

Kaolin clays have very few or no mineral impurities and are thus used for porcelain works. Kaolin clays tend to fire into very light grey, white, or off-white colors. Despite how beautiful these types usually are, kaolin clay isn't very plastic and is very hard to work with, which is why porcelain is so expensive. It also fires at temperatures that far exceed those of stoneware and fire clay. Potters often mix other clay into kaolin clay to make it easier to work with and to lower the temperature it needs to be fired at. In many cases, a porcelain body is a mixture of kaolin and ball clay.

There are various types of glazes throughout the world, often determined by color and texture, but there are a few other very important properties that are looked at when it comes to glazes, especially in terms of appearance.

Opacity

This refers to the glaze's ability to let light pass through it, or in simpler terms, how see-through the glaze is. If a glaze is completely solid and you can't see through it at all, the glaze is called opaque, while a completely clear glaze is called transparent. Translucent is a term that refers to a glaze that is neither fully transparent or fully opaque, but somewhere in between. There are many uses and effects for these glazes. Opaque glazes are most commonly used as base colors and for painting on designs and patterns. Transparent glazes are most commonly used as a top coat to seal the design, create unity, or add depth. It is also the best option if you want your glaze to waterproof your work. Translucent glazes are the best way to create new colors through layering and can have some interesting effects when used creatively.

Reflection

Everything reflects light, and the intensity of this reflection determines if something is gloss or matte. The more light the glaze reflects, the glossier your glaze will be. Matte, on the other hand, reflects much less light. Matte and gloss glaze can be used to get some really great effects, especially if used in combination, but keep in mind that if you use a gloss clear glaze as a top coat on a piece that has a matte glaze, you will lose the matte effect to some extent. The same goes for using a matte clear glaze over a very glossy glaze. A clear matte glaze is the absolute best option if you want to seal or waterproof your clay while altering the appearance of the clay as little as possible. Satin refers to a glaze that is somewhere between a gloss and matte.

Texture

Although most glazes are generally smooth, many glazes are created to give a specific texture to your work, such as glazes that form cracks or ripples as they dry, or more subtle textures that are just a little grainy or rough. Textures are a great way to add to the look of your work, and you can even combine different textures. The thickness of your glaze also has an impact on the texture of your gloss, and a thin glaze works better if you want to keep the texture of the clay intact as long as possible. You can also use thicker layers of glaze to fill in unwanted texture in your clay. This will, however, take longer to dry, and it will affect the color greatly, especially if you're using a more transparent glaze.

Color

This is the property potters look at the most when choosing a glaze. There's an extremely large variety of colors available on the market, and an infinite selection if you're making your own. Some glazes are created to work with a slight gradient effect, which contains small particles of other colors or minerals that react differently than the rest of the glaze when fired so that you have a multi-colored effect from a single glaze. Glazes can also be mixed together to make new colors, or you can mix your own colors once you understand the basics of powdered glaze recipes. There are almost no limits to the color range of your glazes, even with transparent or translucent glazes, beyond your own creativity.

Chapter 2
Stains and Oxides in a Glaze

Oxides and stains are a great way to play with the color and texture of your work. These two are very similar, but they do have some differences.

Stains are a type of glaze designed specifically to emulate the fired color. Unlike regular glazes and oxides, the stain won't l change color as it fires. Stains are also a bit safer to use than oxides, as they contain fewer toxic chemicals and can create almost precisely the same result every time when mixed with water. It's also easier to fine-tune the exact shade and hue you want. Stains may be a bit more expensive than regular glazes and oxides, and they tend to be a little more difficult to dissolve in water, but they can save you a great deal of time and effort, which can be an exceptional help. Stains can be applied using the same techniques as regular glazes. Stains can even be mixed with glazes for a thicker substance.

Stains are created by melting ceramic oxides and coloring oxides together in a kiln.

This mixture is then quenched and ground into a fine powder. These powders are then mixed with organic colorants and dissolved in water to form a stain. Because the oxides have already been fired once, they have already undergone the chemical reaction that comes from exposure to heat and will not change color when firing the pot. The stain powder can be used in regular glaze recipes as a colorant as well as being used on its own. You can also use a stain over dried layers of glaze, or use glaze over dried stains. Stains can also be applied fairly thin to help maintain the texture of your clay.

Oxides are one of the main ways to color your glaze, and often form the basis around specific color recipes. However, oxides are very different from glazes. Glazes are a mixture of different chemicals and compounds, usually with a high silica content, but oxides are made up of one single component, which is usually metal based. Oxides are one of the easiest ways to cover your piece easily in a solid color, as the oxides won't move to fill deeper spaces and form natural highlights during firing the way glazes do. Oxides can often cause a chemical reaction when exposed to heat, and as such, your glaze may have become a completely different color after glazing. This can be used to your advantage, but it needs to be tested and taken into consideration in your planning.

To use oxides, you will need to create an oxide wash. To do this, simply mix a little bit of your oxide powder with water. Oxides have very strong color pigments, so you will only need a small amount of oxide. You may need to experiment with the oxide to water ratio to find the right intensity of color. The ratio results in a very thin and watery mixture, making it a wash rather than a glaze. The wash will dry much quicker than a glaze and isn't applied as thick. Oxide washes will also result in a dry, matte look for your work and will not help waterproof your earthenware pieces. When using oxides, you need to stir your wash very often, as the oxide particles are heavy and will separate from the water and settle on the bottom of your container very quickly. Otherwise, oxide washes can be applied using the same basic application methods as glazes, such as painting, dipping, wax resists, etc.

One great advantage of oxides and oxide washes is that you can use them to greatly enhance the details in your bisqueware. Normally, the oxide wash will coat your piece evenly and result in a solid color, making it hard to make out any details. But you can use a cloth or piece of paper towel to gently wipe over the piece. This will remove a bit of the pigment from the raised surfaces while leaving all the pigment in the deeper areas like carved lines and corners. This will also help remove excess wash that may run while firing and fuse to your kiln shelf. Raw clay will absorb the wash a little more than bisqueware, meaning the effect will be a little less intense, but the technique still works on both raw and bisqued clay. If you want to strengthen your effect, simply use a fine brush to add more wash to the areas you want darker and wipe over the piece again. You can also add more layers to your piece. It will be more effective if you let the first layer of wash dry slightly, and remember that the wash will take longer to dry on the areas where it's thicker. Oxides can also be mixed into your glaze to get a similar effect, as the oxides will settle in the deeper areas as the glaze dries.

Oxides face similar application problems to glazes, such as oily fingerprints or bisqueware that has been over-fired and become partially waterproof. Another minor problem is that you can end up with fingerprints where you hold your piece while applying the oxides, especially when dipping the piece. Luckily, there are cheap, easy to come by tools such as finger sheaths or tongs that can help you solve this problem.

Another great use of oxides is to create patinas. A patina is a thin layer of wash or stain that adds color to the work, while still keeping the texture of the clay itself visible. This can result in very beautiful and interesting pieces, and is very easy to apply in a few simple steps:

1. Bisque your work and let it cool before applying a patina, as raw clay will absorb the patina too much.

2. Mix your patina, wash, or stain, and moisten an old sponge.

3. Working in small sections at a time, apply your patina in a thick layer.

4. Before your patina dries, gently rub the patina off your work, making sure you remove as much as possible. By applying your patina very thick, you will force the color into the pores that create the texture, which will not be removed, emphasizing the texture.

5. Keep repeating steps 3–4 until your entire pot is covered.

6. Let the patina dry. Add a layer of clear glaze if you want.

7. Fire your pot.

Patina is a great way to add an aging effect to your work, and can easily be applied over another dried stain or oxide wash, or even a glaze if they've been applied thinly enough.

Chapter 3
Underglaze wash

Underglazing is a technique that refers to applying glazes to create decorative designs and images on the surface of your clay, be it a simple, repeating pattern of lines and dots, or an intricate work of art. Underglazes refer to the materials applied to the clay, such as colored glazes, slips, stains, etc. There are, however, glazes that have been created specifically for underglazing, which is called an underglaze. You also get more specialized tools, such as underglaze pens that can make applying an underglaze easier and more convenient. There are also many recipes for making your own glazes.

Although all application techniques are suitable, the most effective and controlled method is still painting. Another great method is to use an underglaze wash. The biggest difference between a glaze and a wash is that a wash is much thinner than a glaze, as a lot more water is used to mix the wash. You can also thin a glaze out a little by adding water to create your own wash. The main use for washes is to bring out the detail and texture in carved and stamped bisqueware, much like oxides and stains. There are a few easy steps to do this.

1. To start off, brush a few layers of the wash onto the bisqueware and let it dry slightly. Many potters prefer to use a sponge rather than a regular brush for this.

2. Using a damp cloth or sponge, wipe off the wash. Make sure you don't use too much pressure and remove all the wash on your clay. You will see that the wash has collected in all the deeper, carved areas of the clay, making them darker and more prominent. The wash will also have left a faint stain on the clay which will be more noticeable.

3. Add new colors of wash if you want and let them dry slightly.

4. Wipe the wash off again, but use significantly less moisture and pressure if you want to keep more of the wash color on your clay. Also be careful not to wipe over the same area too often, as the moisture will make the lower layer of wash wet again and muddy the colors.

5. Bisque the pot again for a few minutes if

you plan on adding glazes to the pot over the wash.

Washes are also great for using stamps on pottery work, and you can get a great watercolor effect when painting with a wash. You can use washes over regular glazes and stains, but if you want to apply a clear glaze over a wash, you need to work carefully and use light brush strokes, as the liquid in the glaze might activate the wash again and drag some of the color and pigment with it as you brush on the glaze.

Chapter 4
Soluble Salts

Soluble salts are minerals, such as magnesium sulfate or calcium, found inside your clay, which will dissolve into your clay once moistened. These soluble salts can have interesting effects on your clay, which can be positive or negative, depending on how you use them. Soluble salts can also be used in your glazes, to create interesting new effects. When using soluble salts in your glazes, the soluble salts will be absorbed into the raw clay or bisqueware, taking the glaze with them and creating a visual effect similar to using watercolors on paper. Most soluble salts are metal by nature, such as chrome, cobalt, and copper.

In essence, you mix a soluble salt with a clear glaze stain or wash. The type of soluble salt will determine the color of your glaze, and the amount will determine the intensity of your color when fired. Glazing with soluble salts works similar to glazing with stains and washes and is most commonly done through painting. Because the soluble salt mixture is so thin and runny, it can be difficult to work with, especially when creating patterns and designs. Because the colors are so thin and translucent, advanced layering is nearly impossible, as you won't be able to properly cover the color underneath. This in itself can be used to your advantage to create interesting new effects. You will also sometimes have to apply several layers of a single salt wash to get a strong color. These soluble salt washes also work best on white clays, meaning you'll use them on stoneware rather than earthenware. This is also a very popular technique to use on porcelain.

To help you get started, here is a list of some of the most common soluble salts and the colors they can give you:

- Barium: light green

- Calcium: red

- Chrome: brown or olive green

- Copper: blue or green

- Lead: pale blue

- Potassium: violet

- Sodium: Yellow

- Strontium: crimson

You may notice that if you mix these powders with your glaze, not all of the glazes match the color described in the list. This is because the salts have a different chemical reaction to heat than water, and as the piece will be fired, the final color of the salt wash will be determined by the chemical reaction of the salt to high temperatures.

The list provided is very basic, and there are many more soluble salts available. These salts can also be combined to create new colors. You will have to experiment a little to find the soluble salts you want to use for this technique. Although the best way to experiment is through test tiles, a quick way to see the type of color you can expect is to expose the salt to heat. You should always be careful when trying this, as most salts are toxic and highly flammable. Here are a few steps you can follow to flame test a soluble salt safely:

1.   To start, make sure you are working in a well-ventilated area. If you need to work outside, make sure your work area is protected from the wind.

2.   You will also need some safety gear and special equipment. For safety gear, you will need safety goggles, oven mitts, and a mask to protect yourself from any noxious fumes and gases. You should also keep a fire extinguisher nearby in case of an

emergency. In terms of equipment, you will need platinum or nichrome wire, hydriodic acid, and a source of flame, such as a Bunsen burner or long fire nozzle lighter.

3. To start, clean your wire with the acid to remove any chemicals that may affect your results. Then dip one end of your wire into the salt you want to test. There should be some acid still attached to the wire to help the salt stick.

4. Working carefully, hold the wire with your salt over your flame until the salt ignites. If you've used a small amount of salt, there will be a sudden flare of colored fire that will disappear again quickly.

5. The color of the flame will tell you the color of a fired glaze made with that salt. Note that if you are using nichrome wire, there will always be a hint of orange in the flame together with the color from the salt.

Always be very careful when working with open flames like this and never do this when there are children or small animals in the vicinity. If you do have a small child and do your ceramic work at home, it's better to test the salt through test tiles alone. Also remember that although the flame test will show you the type of color the salt will create, the salt will still react to the other ingredients of the glaze and the minerals in your clay, so the final results may still be a little different. As such, you should still test each soluble salt glaze before using on your piece to prevent ruining days of hard work and patience.

If you're mixing salts, you should keep in mind that they have chemical reactions to each other as well, and they may not have the color you expect once fired. This is also a technique where you have to try it out and experiment a little before you decide if you like it or not.

Chapter 5
Glaze Layering

Glaze layering is a technique that involves applying several layers of glaze and underglaze over each other to create an image, design, or visual effect on your pottery. This technique can help bring more depth and realism into any work and is fairly simple and straightforward once you understand what to do. In essence, you apply one layer of colored glazes, let it dry, and add the next layer. Keep adding layers until your design or image is complete. You may also want to layer a few layers of the same color over each other to make the color more solid and intense.

Although layering is simple in its essence, there are a few things that should always be taken into consideration. First is the order of your layers, as each layer will cover the next. You need to plan out which layer is further in the back and which is further to the front, as the back layers will be "behind" the layers to the front. To help illustrate my point, I will use the example of a butterfly on a flower, in front of a patterned background. The first layer would be the base color, followed by the pattern. Next is the flower, and the butterfly would be last, as it's in front of the flower.

Something else to take into consideration is that some colors cover better than others, and it is easier to layer dark colors over white colors rather than the other way around. Some colors, like white and yellow, are especially difficult to work with as they don't cover other colors well and take several layers to do so. When planning your layers, you should always think carefully about which colors you are going to put on top of each other.

Here's a simple guide on how to do layering, using the same example of a butterfly on a flower:

1. Cover the area with your base color. Depending on the object, a dip might be most effective.

2. Let the base color dry completely. Use a glaze or wash to add the background pattern. Let this layer dry completely.

3. Paint the base color of the stem of the flower. You can add some shading and highlights here.

4. Let the layer dry again and add some more details to the stem, such as shadows from

the petals, etc. You can also use semi-transparent glazes to do some darker and lighter gradients. Let this layer dry.

5. Paint the base colors of the petals and the center of the flower and let them dry completely. Add some details and shading.

6. Paint the base colors of the butterfly once the previous layer is done. Let it dry and add details to the wings.

7. Once that layer is dry, you can add some final details to the whole thing, such as super highlights and outlines.

8. If you want, you can add a layer of clear glaze over the whole design to give the piece a more uniform look.

9. Fire the piece once the last layer has been completed. If you intend to repeat the design several times across your piece, you can do the same layer of each design at once, i.e. the base color for all the stems, then the details for all the stems, then the base color for the flower petals, etc. This can make your work go much faster than repeating the same process for each design.

Cone 6 Glaze Recipes

Here are two recipes for glazes that are excellent for layering, and need to be fired at cone 6, or mid-range temperatures. Cone 6 is one of the best glaze types for layering as the colors are usually vibrant and the layers work well when placed over one another.

Glaze recipes are usually written down in percentages, to make it easier to adapt the size of a batch. As an example, a recipe may contain 30% silica. In a 100 g batch, that means you would use 30 g silica, while in a 500 g batch you would use 150 g silica.

Chameleon Glaze

Soda feldspar: 46.73%

EPK kaolin: 18.68%

Talk: 14.02%

Zinc oxide: 9.35%

Whiting: 9.35%

Lithium carbonate: 1.87%

This is a dark gray glaze, but becomes lighter shades of reddish-brown when applied thinly. This glaze is also very dark when applied to porcelain. The glaze also becomes more matte depending on how thick you apply it. You can add 2.80% copper carbonate for a slightly altered color.

Chun Glaze

Soda feldspar: 36.54%

Silica: 32.69%

Whiting: 13.46%

Zinc oxide: 11.54%

Ball clay: 5.77%

This is a light green glaze that works great with layering and can be thinned out for washes or lighter colors. The glaze also becomes fairly dark when applied in thick layers. You can add 0.58% copper carbonate for a slight alteration in color.

Cone 10 Glaze Recipes

Cone 10 is also a very popular temperature for glaze layering, as most stoneware is glazed at cone 10, and glazes created for lower temperatures will overheat and discolor. Cone 10 glazes also tend to react to each other on a chemical level very well and are great for layering in general.

Blue Celadon Glaze

Cluster feldspar: 40%

Silica: 35%

Barium carbonate: 8%

Whiting: 7%

Strontium carbonate: 5%

EPK kaolin: 5%

This is a very strong blue glaze that is fairly matte but does have some gloss to it. You can add 0.5% bentonite or 1.5% Spanish red iron oxide for some slight color variations.

Pier Black Glaze

Cluster feldspar: 43%

Dolomite: 24%

EPK kaolin: 23%

Whiting: 5%

Borax: 5%

This is a very lovely black glaze that works great to add gradients and shading to darken the colors already on your pot. You can add 6.6% cobalt carbonate or 6.6% iron chromate for a slight variation in the hue of thin layers of this glaze.

Chapter 6
Luster Glazing

Luster glazing refers to the technique where a special overglaze is applied over a glazed and fired piece, which gives the piece a very beautiful look, and can bring a piece to a whole new level. Luster glazes come in many different colors and metallic effects, but the most common use for luster glazing is with gold luster.

Gold Luster

In essence, a gold luster glaze consists of very fine particles of gold, suspended in a liquid such as pine oil resin — it must be organic. When applied, the glaze may look a little thin and uneven, but once the piece is fired again it will look more solid. Gold luster may be a little too expensive to cover every pot you make completely, but it's great for decorative accents and patterns. Something to keep in mind is that it is possible to apply luster too thick or thin. If a luster glaze is too thick, it will likely bubble or tear when firing. It can also drip when applied too thick to a vertical surface. If it's applied too thin, your luster will look streaky, or have a purple color after firing, rather than a full, rich gold. You should also keep in mind that the luster will take on some of the properties of the surface it's applied to, so if you apply it over a smooth, glossy glaze the luster will be smoother and glossier too. If you apply the luster to a matte, textured glaze, the luster will be more matte and textured as well.

Applying gold luster is very simple and easy, and can be done in a few steps.

1. Glaze and properly fire your ceramic piece. Let it cool before proceeding to the next step.

2. Make sure your surface is clean of any dust or oily residue, as that might prevent the overglaze from sticking to your piece.

3. Apply the glaze to all the areas you want to be accented or decorated with gold luster. The best tool to use for this is a brush to paint on the luster.

4. Make sure you don't touch the gold luster while it's still wet, as that might leave marks when firing.

5. Let your luster dry for about 24 hours before firing.

6. Fire the piece according to the instructions

of the luster. Let it cool properly before removing it from the kiln.

Firing a gold luster is fairly simple and straightforward, and it's not that different from firing a glaze. One of the big differences is that gold luster releases strong noxious fumes while firing that can leak from the kiln and cause severe headaches. Because of this, you should make sure that your kiln is a fair distance away from your living space and in a well-ventilated area. Lusters should also be fired at lower temperatures than the firing temperatures of your glaze. If you fire the luster glaze at a high temperature, you may risk over firing the piece and causing damage to your initial glaze. Make sure you read the instructions of your specific gold luster brand very carefully to make sure you fire it at the right temperature for the right amount of time.

Chapter 7
Decals

Decals are a great tool for applying patterns, especially if you're making a set of pieces that all have the same pattern. A decal is a pattern or image that has been printed using special ink and paper so that the image can be transferred onto a ceramic work. Decals work similar to an underglaze, in that they are applied over a glazed, fired piece, and fired or heated a third time (second time if your piece has not been bisqued) to seal the decal into the glaze.

Initially, there are two types of decals: heat transfer and water transfer. Both methods are fairly easy to use and are placed over pieces that have already been glazed and fired. Here are the instructions for applying both types of decal to your ceramic works:

Heat Transfer Decal

As the name implies, this type of decal uses dry heat to melt an adhesive attached to the decal and let it adhere to the ceramic glaze instead.

1.   The first step to applying a decal is to make

sure the decal fits onto your piece. You should also trim the paper around the decal to make it easier to place the design precisely where you want it.

2. Your decal will be on a carrier sheet of plastic. Place the decal on your ceramic piece, with the decal in direct contact with the ceramic piece.

3. Make sure your decal stays in place. This is fairly easy when using a flat, horizontal surface, but it may be a bit difficult on vertical or curved surfaces. You will have to hold it in place yourself, and you will need oven mitts to protect your hands from the heat.

4. Using a heat gun, expose the decal to the highest setting of heat for short intervals. Keep the heat gun two or three inches away from the decal when exposing the heat, and make sure you don't expose the decal to heat for more than five seconds at a time. If you expose the decal to too much heat at once, your plastic carrier sheet will begin to melt and shrink, which will warp your decal.

5. After every five seconds of heat exposure, use a credit card or firm, dry sponge to make sure the decal is completely smooth

and flat against your piece.

6.   Keep applying heat at five second intervals until your decal has adhered fully to your piece. For smaller decals, five or six cycles should be enough (more for larger pieces). Very large pieces might need to be adhered to the piece in sections.

7.   Once your decal is completely adhered, let the piece cool fully before using it.

8.   As an optional step, some potters like to cover the decal with a clear glaze and firing it again, to make sure the decal is sealed onto the piece properly. If you want to do this, you need to make sure you have the right decal and glaze, as some decals might not be able to withstand the extremely high temperatures required to melt some glazes.

Water Transfer Decal

A water decal, also often called a side decal, uses water to activate an adhesive and remove it from the paper backing. The piece is then fired at extremely low temperatures to seal the decal to the glaze.

1.   Once again, make sure that your decal fits onto your piece. You may also want to trim the paper backing around the decal to

make placement easier.

2. Using a damp sponge, moisten the decal until it separates slightly from the paper backing. The edges of the decal will start to curl away from the paper backing.

3. Making sure your ceramic piece is clean of any dust or oily residues, place the decal in the right position. Folding the paper backing back a little, press one of the edges of the decal to your piece and carefully slide the paper backing out from under the decal.

4. Working very carefully, as the decal is very fragile, you can slide the decal around over the surface to make sure the decal is in exactly the right position you want.

5. Use a damp sponge to smooth out all the bubbles under your decal. Remember to work carefully so you don't tear the decal. Once all the bubbles are gone, carefully dab the decal with paper towels to remove excess water from under the decal.

6. Let the decal dry completely. If you do discover any more bubbles, use a pin to gently break the bubble, moisten the area with a bit of water, and smooth it out. Let that area dry again.

7. Once completely dry, fire the piece according to the instructions of your decal. These decals are fired at very low temperatures, usually around cone 015.

8. Let cool completely before removing from the kiln.

Most decals aren't dishwasher safe, even after firing, so make sure you read the instructions of your decal before applying the decal to any dishes.

Although decals are fairly cheap and easy to come by, you are limited by what is available in the store. Luckily, it's very simple to make your own decals with a few specialized tools. The most important of which is decal paper, which can be bought from stores or ordered online. Simply use a laser printer to print your desired image onto the decal paper. You can then apply this decal as you would a regular water transfer decal. You can use any images you want but here are a few websites where you can get specifically designed decal images to get you started:

https://www.vecteezy.com/free-vector/decals

https://www.freepik.com/free-photos-vectors/decals

Chapter 8
China Paints

China painting refers to the technique of creating designs or patterns, through layering, on a piece that has already been glazed and fired. As the name implies, this technique is especially used for china pieces. The paints used for this technique are specially designed to act as an overglaze so they stick to the glass-like surface of the glazed work. These overglazes are called china paints and are made from ground minerals and a compound called flux, a finely ground type of glass similar to porcelain, which will melt when firing and fuse to the fired glaze. These powder mixes are the most common form in which they are sold. Potters then mix the powders with water or other liquids into a very thin paint. Ideally, the china paints are applied as a wash, meaning that a single bottle of china paint will last you fairly long. As the name implies, the most common application technique for this is painting.

China paints are fairly expensive, especially colors like purple and red which contain traces of gold. You don't want to waste it by using cheap application tools. Cheap, hard brushes can be very streaky and uneven. Cheap brushes also tend to lose hairs, which can be difficult to remove from the painted image. You'll want good quality tools that can help you reach the ultimate potential of china paints. There are tools on the market tailored for china painting, but these are expensive. If you're still new to the craft and still experimenting, you may not be ready to commit fully yet. It's best to buy a set of good quality brushes to begin with. It may still be a little pricey, but if you decide china painting isn't for you, you can use the brushes for luster glazes or underglazing.

As mentioned, the powders are mixed with liquids. There are different types of liquids that can be used for this, although oils are the suggested mediums, such as pine oil, pen oil, or baby oil. Different oils have different reactions, such as baby oil, that never completely dry and is good for mixing large batches that can be stored for later, or pen oil that is great for thinning out your paint without letting it run or bleed. Different oils dry at different speeds, provide different textures and thicknesses, and different feels to the brush strokes. For those who are allergic to oils or don't enjoy using them, there are water-based mediums you can use. The medium you use will disintegrate during firing, so which medium you use depends purely on your preferences. The best way to find out what you like is to experiment with a few small batches using different mediums. To start off, however, you should follow the instructions provided with your china paints to familiarize yourself with the technique first.

China painting is applied just like regular underglazes, and layering works great if you use a medium that dries. Firing is also similar to other overglazes. These paints are usually fired around cone 015 to 018, but always follow the firing instructions of your specific brand of china paints. Always remember to let your piece cool completely before removing it from the kiln.

Something that might be a little troublesome with china paints is cleaning brushes. The oil and minerals of the paints tend to stick to your brushes, and a simple rinse in water won't be enough to clean your brushes properly. To get rid of the oil, you will need to use solvents, such as turpentine or acetone. However, be careful not to use harsh solvents that will damage your brushes.

Chapter 9
Triaxial Blend

Triaxial blending is a method of testing three coloring ingredients and their combinations for ceramic glazes.

For this method, you will end up with at least six glazes, each in a slightly different color. The triaxial blend tests how each of the coloring ingredients work on their own and in combination with each other. It can also be used to test color mixing.

1. To start, let's label the ingredients as *ingredient A,* which will result in a red color, *ingredient B,* which will result in a blue color, and *ingredient C,* which will result in a yellow color.

2. Mix each coloring ingredient with a bit of glaze. The best way to test these glazes is to use a test tile. Place the three test tiles of the glazes in a triangle.

3. Next, mix three more glazes. In the first glaze, add one part ingredient A and one part ingredient B—this should result in a

purple glaze. Place the test tile of this glaze in the triangle between glaze A and B. Divide the size of each part so that the total of the added ingredients is the same as the amount of the single ingredient you've added to the glazes.

4. Add 1 part ingredient B and 1 part ingredient C to mix a glaze. Create a test tile—which should be green—and place it in the triangle between ingredients B and C.

5. Repeat this process with ingredients A and C—which should result in an orange test tile—and complete the triangle. This way, you can see how the ingredients react to each other and make comparisons. The Triangle should look as follows:

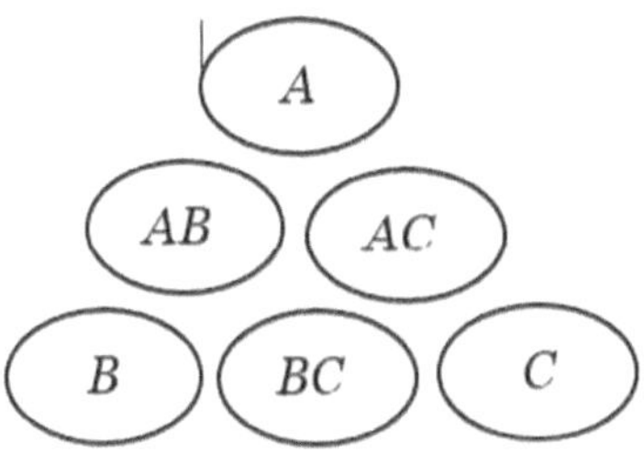

6. You can also increase the size of the triangle to test more reactions. Create a triangle where you test two reactions for

each leg between the ingredients. Test the ingredients by adding two parts ingredient A and one part ingredient B to one glaze, and one part ingredient A and two parts ingredient B in another. Place these two test tiles between ingredients one and two in the triangle. This time you will need to divide the size of the ingredients by three to maintain the percentage balance in your glaze.

7. Repeat this with ingredients B and C, and A and C. You should now have nine test tiles in total.

8. To complete the triangle, add one part ingredient A, one part ingredient B, and one part ingredient C to a glaze and place the test tile for that glaze in the center of the circle. The triangle should look like this:

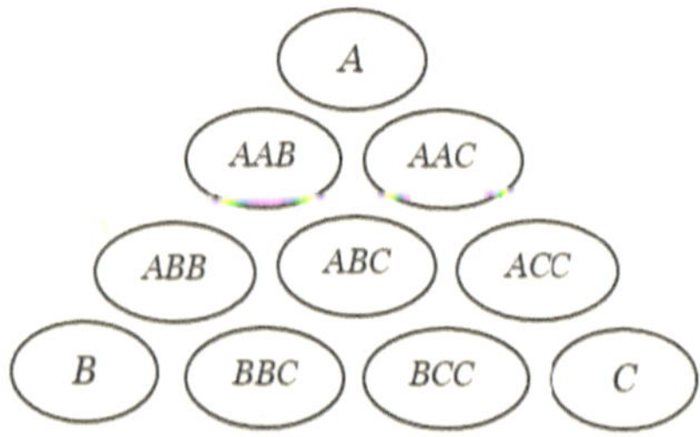

9. Fire all your test tiles and reassemble your triangle so you can compare the final

results.

Although I've used the three primary colors for this example, you can use any combination of the three ingredients or colors. The point of this test is to experiment with combinations and compare them to each other. This is great for fine-tuning your own recipes to find the perfect combination for what you want.

You can increase the size of the triangle even more, though it will be a little more complicated. If, for example, you want to create a triangle with five glazes in each leg, you will make three glazes for each color combination, in order of two parts A and one part B, one part A and one part B, and one part A and two parts B. This will be repeated for every glaze. In the center, you will have three glazes instead of one, which will be a little more complicated to mix. For the glaze closest to glaze A, you will need to mix two parts A, one part B, and one part C. For the glaze closest to glaze B you will mix one part A, two parts B, and one part C. For the glaze closest to C, you will mix one part A, one part B, and two parts C. Your triangle will look like this:

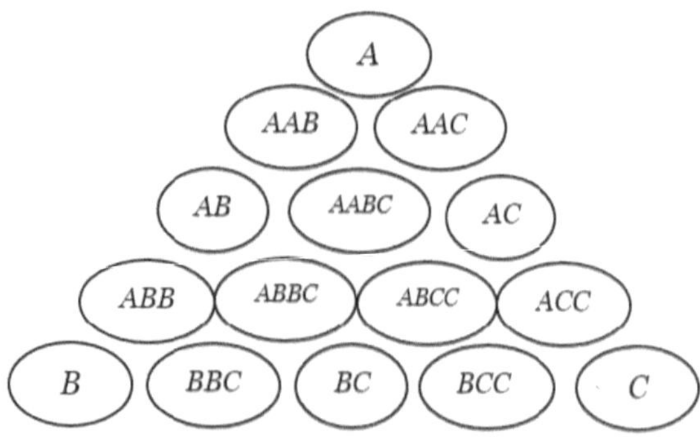

For glazes that consist of 2 parts, like *AB*, *BC*, and *AC*, you should divide the size of each part by two. For pieces that consist of three parts, like *AAB*, *AAC*, and *ABB*, you should divide the size of each part by three. For glazes that consist of four parts, like *AABC*, *ABBC*, and *ABCC*, you should divide the size of each part by for. You can also think of it in terms of halves and thirds; one part A and one part B can also be ½ part A and ½ part B, or one part A and two parts B can be ⅓ part A and ⅔ part B.

By now you have hopefully noticed a pattern that forms as you increase the size of your triangle. By using this pattern, you can increase the number of combinations to test and compare by adding more glazes to each leg of the triangle.

Just as when you do a regular glaze test, you should label your test tiles accurately, as they won't stay in the triangle while firing, and keep careful notes of your results. You might also want to take a photo of your fired test tiles placed in your triangle, so you don't have to repeat the whole process again if you want to review your results in the future, but have sold a few of the test tiles.

Chapter 10
Specific Gravity

The term *specific gravity* is a unit that determines the consistency of a material by using the mass of a predetermined volume of said material and comparing it to the mass of the same volume of water. In ceramics, the specific mass is used to determine the thickness of a glaze, wash, underglaze, etc. There is special equipment that can be used to measure specific gravity, but there is a very simple formula you can use to measure specific gravity that won't cost you anything. This formula is the weight of the material divided by the volume of the material. As an example, 100 ml water weighs 100 g, meaning, if you divide the weight by the volume, you will have a specific gravity of 1. If you have a 100 ml glaze that weighs 150g, that glaze will have a specific gravity of 1.5.

The theory of this works simple enough, but you may not want to use a full 100 ml of glaze to find out the specific gravity, which can make it a little more difficult to work out the specific gravity. Here are some basic steps you can follow to measure the specific gravity of your glazes.

1. First and foremost, you will need a gram scale and a container in which you are going to weigh your glaze.

2. If you have an electric gram scale that can balance the scale to zero once you've placed the container on it, you can skip this step and move to the next. Otherwise, weigh your container and write it down on a piece of paper. Keep that paper close by, as you will need it later.

3. Measure the right amount of glaze into the container—I will be using the example of 20 ml for these instructions—and weigh the glaze.

4. If you weren't able to balance your scale to 0 after placing the empty container on it, subtract the weight of the empty container from the total weight, otherwise skip to the next step. As an example, your total weight is 234 g, but your container weighs 200 g, If you subtract the weight of your container, your glaze itself will weigh 34 g.

5. Divide the weight of glaze by the volume, i.e. 20 in this case, to find the specific gravity of your glaze. Round numbers such

as 30, 40, 60, etc. are fairly easy to calculate off the top of your head, especially if you have an easy volume to work with, but for less ideal weights you may want to use a calculator for this. In the case of the example I've provided, your formula will be 34 divided by 20, meaning your specific gravity will be 1.7.

6. Make sure to keep track of your specific gravity and write it down for later use.

7. If you're measuring the specific gravity of several glazes in one sitting, make sure you properly clean and dry the container before moving on to the next glaze, as any glaze or water that stays behind can influence the weight of your glaze and lead to an inaccurate reading and your specific gravity will be wrong. This is especially problematic if you're using small volumes of glaze. You can also use a different container for each glaze, but you will have to balance your scale or weigh your container each time you switch containers.

Now that you know how to measure specific gravity, it's time you know why it's important to know what the specific gravity of your glaze is. The main reason why you want to measure the specific gravity is to make sure your glaze is the right consistency—meaning it isn't too thick or too runny—for what you want to do with it. Dipping glazes usually have slightly lower specific gravity than glazes used for painting, while washes have much lower specific gravity than most other glazes. This is a much more accurate indication of what the consistency of your glaze should be than telling you the glaze should be as thick as milk, heavy cream, or pancake batter, as these can be relative. Some packages of powder glaze mix will tell you what the estimated specific gravity should be, and can be a great guide for beginners who haven't mastered the art of finding the right consistency by looking at the glaze.

Specific gravity is also great for making sure all the glazes you mix are all the same consistency, which can save you a lot of time, effort, and material. If you have different colors of the same brand and type of glaze mix, you can use the specific gravity to make sure that all your glazes are the same consistency. This is especially important if you plan on doing designs, images, or layering, since using a glaze that is thicker or thinner than the others can influence your application technique, and is usually also visible after firing. Specific gravity is also great for when you've mixed a batch of glaze that ends up not being enough, and you have to mix more. Rather than mixing and trying to match the new batch to the old batch by visually comparing the consistencies and testing them both, mix a batch of glaze with the same specific gravity as the previous batch.

To help you get started with this measurement technique, here are some rough averages of the specific gravity of different glaze types. Keep in mind that some ingredient materials, especially metals, are heavier than others, and can influence what your specific gravity should be.

- Dipping glazes: 1.5–1.7

- Brushing glazes: 1.45–1.60

- Spraying glazes: 1.7–2

- Washes and stains: 1.05–1.3

- Overglazes such as luster glazes should have the same specific gravity as brushing glazes, while china paint needs a specific gravity that matches those of washes and stains.

Chapter 11
Tips and Tricks

Techniques are all good and well, but it's still easy to make a few mistakes due to ignorance and or carelessness. A few good habits, a little extra knowledge, and a hint of cleverness can help you save money, time, prevent mistakes, and bring your ceramic work to a new level in an easy and simple way. Here are 10 useful tips and tricks to help make your ceramic work look more professional:

1. **Test everything:** Even if you buy premade glazes, mix packages of glaze mix, or create your own glaze recipes, always test everything to make sure you know what you're working with. The material you are using may not exactly match the image on the packaging, or it may not look exactly like you remember it. Even if the color is the same, you may mix it to a slightly different consistency or you may use a different application technique. All of this can have an effect on your final result. Use test tiles. Use the triaxial blend and

specific gravity to help you make sure you have what you're looking for, and keep thorough records of all your tests, to help lessen the amount of testing you will have to do next time. It doesn't matter if you're using a regular glaze, soluble salt, stain, wash, luster glaze, china paint or a decal, you should still do a sample test. You should also test your clay, as well as any glazing techniques you plan on using to see if the techniques will work with the glaze and clay you're using and to see if the technique will give you the results you're looking for.

2. **Keep your brushes exclusive:** When I say this, I mean that you should have a specific set of brushes for every technique or materials you're going to use. If you use three brushes for applying a luster glaze, you shouldn't use those brushes for china paints or applying underglazes. At a quick glance, it may seem more economical to have one set of good quality brushes that you use for everything, but different materials and application techniques all have different chemical influences on your brush bristles and different cleaning methods. Combining these different reactions and methods can cause damage

and put your brushes under a lot of strain, and it won't be long before you'll need to replace them. If you keep a set of brushes for each material and method, the brushes will become better accustomed and tailored to the hardships associated with it. That way the brushes won't take on as much damage in the long run and you will also prevent overusing your brushes. This concept also works with any other application tools you want to use. If you follow this tip and take good care of your equipment in general, you can keep using the same brushes for years.

3. **Keep your layers thin:** Despite what many say, thick layers of glaze aren't always the way to go. One of the big problems is that thick layers of glaze take a very long time to dry, and they tend to be streaky. The thicker your layer of glaze, the fewer layers you can add before the piece looks bulky, and the best way to get rid of brush strokes is to use several layers painted in different directions. Overall, it's much quicker and easier to apply several thin layers rather than a few thick layers, which results in a much neater finish. Another problem is that thick layers of glaze also cover the texture of your clay,

which many potters like to keep. This can be an especially big problem if you've carved fine, intricate details into your clay before you bisque, and if your glaze layers are too thick, most of this carving work will be lost. Also, if a layer is too thick, it can become heavy and peel off your previous layer of glaze. This can be very difficult to fix, and might permanently ruin your piece completely.

4. **Have a feather touch:** While on the subject of applying glazes, you should always hold your brush lightly when painting a glaze onto your piece. Pressing too hard while painting on a glaze will just push the glaze around, and won't dispense it evenly. You can even end up scratching or picking up the previous layer of glaze, which, once again, is difficult to blend. In severe cases, you can dent greenware if you apply too much pressure. You should also be careful of very delicate clays, like porcelain, which are easy to break when they've been properly fired. Porcelain that has only been bisqued is even more fragile, and applying too much pressure could shatter your piece. Furthermore, a light touch also tends to leave fewer brush strokes, gives you more control over your

brush, and tends to have a cleaner and neater finish than a heavier touch.

5. **Use a whisk and ladle:** If you've made large batches of glaze that you store for later, there's a big chance that a large amount of your glaze has separated, leaving you with a muddy mixture at the bottom and colored water on top. You will have to give the glaze a good stir to mix the ingredients again. The best way to do this is to use a whisk. Whisk your glaze the same way you would whisk baking ingredients together. This might make your arm a little tired, but it's worth it. After whisking, there might still be some bigger chunks stuck to the bottom of your container. Use a ladle to scoop them up into the mixture again. Then use your whisk again to get rid of the last few clumps and mix everything together. Once again, keep tip number two in mind. Don't use the ladle and whisk for anything other than this purpose.

6. **Keep your glazes separate:** It's important to make sure your glazes don't accidentally mix. Because glazes are chemicals, a single drop of a different glaze can ruin your whole container of glaze in more ways than just changing the color.

Unlike regular paint, you can't just scoop out the drop of foreign glaze, the surrounding glaze, and use the rest of the glaze as the chemical process has already started and can't be undone. There are a few simple things you can do to prevent this. Firstly, if you are working with one glaze, make sure that all your other containers of glaze are sealed tightly. Secondly, work with one glaze at a time, and wash your hands and application tools thoroughly before moving on to the next glaze. Thirdly, if you're working in a studio or classroom together with other people, make sure there is enough distance between your work areas so that there is no way to contaminate any glazes. If that is impossible, let the other person finish glazing before starting to glaze yourself.

7. **Always wipe the base:** As mentioned many times before, any glaze that comes into contact with the kiln shelf will fuse to it and ruin the shelf and the piece. As such, you should always make sure the base is clear of any glaze. The simplest and easiest way to do this is to use a damp sponge or cloth to wipe any glaze off the base. You need to be very thorough when doing this, and be careful not to remove any glaze

where you don't want to. Most potters like to use a wax resist on the base. This works great, but you should still gently wipe the base in case there are areas on the base you may have missed with the resist. It is especially important to wipe the base if you've dipped the piece.

8.   **Heat up the piece:** Many potters have discovered that heating the piece in the microwave for half a minute makes the glazing much easier. The glaze stays softer for longer while applying, making the brush slide smoother over the clay. The heat also helps the glaze stick to the clay better. This trick works especially well when working with china.

9.   **Keep your hands clean:** You can never wash your hands enough when glazing ceramics. Any oil or residue stuck to your piece will create a space where your glaze doesn't adhere to the clay, and your glaze will peel and chip off before you can fire the glaze. The same goes for oily spots between layers of glaze. The main source of these oils and residues are your hands. Every time you touch your piece with oily hands, you create a spot where the glaze won't stick. That is why it is so important to make sure your hands are always clean when

handling your piece. Many think that they should use a sanitizer to save time, but that won't work. In some cases, sanitizers contain trace elements of oil that can stick to your glaze or the strong chemicals in the sanitizer can cause an unexpected reaction with your glaze. The only way to keep your hands clean is with soap and water, and make sure that you've rinsed off all the soap afterward.

10. **Always clean your clay:** Even when handling your clay with perfectly clean hands, you aren't necessarily ready to begin glazing yet. While drying and bisque firing, your piece may have gathered some dust, ash, or dirt, that can either prevent your glaze from sticking or cause flaws in your glaze. Wipe your piece with a clean damp cloth, and then with a clean dry cloth, to remove any unwanted dust and dirt. If you've decided to use an old piece you've never glazed, or had a coffee mishap, there's a big chance that you have some stains in the clay. Even if you could get past the glaze not sticking part, the stains can have a severe effect on the color of your glaze, especially when working on light clays. Luckily, cleaners, such as Mr. Clean Magic Erasers are great for removing

tough stains from your clay.

Conclusion

Hopefully, this book has been a great help, and you've learned a few new techniques that will improve the quality of your ceramic glazes. All these techniques are simple once you understand them, and easy to master with a little time and effort. I have done my very best to make this book as straightforward and comprehensible as possible, and encourage you to experiment with the knowledge I have given you. The purpose of this book is to enable and help you learn a few more skills to use in future projects, which can hopefully make your career as a ceramic artist a little more vibrant and diverse.

References

Big Ceramic Store. (2001). Decorating with Ceramic Decals. Retrieved from https://bigceramicstore.com/pages/info-ceramics-tips-tip43_ceramic_decals

Blattenberger, M. (n.d.). A Beginner's Lesson in China Painting. Retrieved from http://www.porcelainpainters.com/ppioclass/beglesson2/page_2.htm

Britt, J. (2018). How to Do a Triaxial Blend to Test Pottery Glazes. Retrieved from https://ceramicartsnetwork.org/daily/ceramic-glaze-recipes/glaze-chemistry/triaxial-blend-test-pottery-glazes/

Britt, J. (2019). Ceramic Stains: The Easy Way to Create All the Colors of the Rainbow on Your Pottery. Retrieved from https://ceramicartsnetwork.org/daily/ceramic-supplies/ceramic-colorants/ceramic-stains-the-easy-way-to-create-all-the-colors-of-the-rainbow-on-your-pottery/

Ceramic Industry. (2000). The Science of Glazing. Retrieved from https://www.ceramicindustry.com/articles/90432-ppp-the-science-of-glazing

Claywork Tutorials: Using Oxides. (n.d.). Retrieved from http://fireverseceramics.weebly.com/using-oxides.html

Craftibles. (n.d.). How to use Heat Transfer Vinyl on Mugs. Retrieved from https://shopcraftables.com/blog/how-to-use-heat-transfer-vinyl-on-mugs/

Earth Nation Ceramics. (2019). *Tips AND tricks for GLAZING [Video]*. Retrieved from https://www.youtube.com/watch?v=6Z4KbKg7iN0&list=PLlrjOezwxajbMr3ydS35jGlvP9S2Es9yN&index=27&t=0s

Hansen, T. (n.d.). Soluble Salts. Retrieved from https://digitalfire.com/4sight/glossary/glossary_soluble_salts.html

Mallory, A. (2015). *Cone 10 Layering Glazes*. Retrieved from https://ceramicartsnetwork.org/ceramics-monthly/ceramic-glaze-recipes/cone-10-layering-glazes/#

Peterson, B. (2019). The Basics of Pottery Clay. Retrieved from https://www.thesprucecrafts.com/clay-basics-2746314

Pier, D. (2019). Using Rare Earth Oxides as Ceramic Colorants to Obtain Intense Colors. Retrieved from https://ceramicartsnetwork.org/daily/ceramic-supplies/ceramic-colorants/using-rare-earth-oxides-as-ceramic-colorants-to-obtain-intense-colors/

Stamps, A. (2018). Two Great Cone 6 Ceramic Glazes that Look Great Layered and On Their Own. Retrieved from https://ceramicartsnetwork.org/daily/ceramic-glaze-recipes/mid-range-glaze-recipes/two-great-cone-6-ceramic-glazes-that-look-great-layered-and-on-their-own/

Tolosa, M. (2018). Pottery Making Illustrated. Retrieved from https://ceramicartsnetwork.org/pottery-making-illustrated/pottery-making-techniques/ceramic-decorating-techniques/luster-101/#

Tulloch, K. (2015). Syracuse China: Ceramic expert offers glazing tips before Sunday's final giveaway. Retrieved from https://www.syracuse.com/entertainment/2015/05/syracuse_china_glazing_tips_for_beginners.html

Wired Chemist. (n.d.). Qualitative Analysis. Retrieved from

http://www.wiredchemist.com/chemistry/inst
ructional/laboratory-tutorials/qualitative-
analysis